UNDERSTANDING A3 THINKING

A Critical Component of Toyota's PDCA Management System

UNDERSTANDING
A3 THINKING

A Critical Component
of Toyota's PDCA
Management System

DURWARD K. SOBEK II AND ART SMALLEY

CRC Press
Taylor & Francis Group
Boca Raton   London   New York

CRC Press is an imprint of the
Taylor & Francis Group, an **informa** business

A PRODUCTIVITY PRESS BOOK

Productivity Press
Taylor & Francis Group
6000 Broken Sound Parkway NW, Suite 300
Boca Raton, FL 33487-2742

© 2008 by Durward K. Sobek II and Art Smalley
Productivity Press is an imprint of Taylor & Francis Group, an Informa business

No claim to original U.S. Government works
Printed in the United States of America on acid-free paper
10 9 8 7 6 5 4 3
International Standard Book Number-13: 978-1-56327-360-5 (Hardcover)

Library of Congress Cataloging-in-Publication Data

Sobek, Durward K.
  Understanding A3 thinking : a critical component of Toyota's PDCA management system / Durward K. Sobek II and Art Smalley.
       p. cm.
  Includes bibliographical references and index.
  ISBN 978-1-56327-360-5 (alk. paper)
  1. Toyota Jidosha Kogyo Kabushiki Kaisha. 2. Production management—Case studies. 3. Industrial productivity. I. Smalley, Art. II. Title.
  TL278.S63 2008
  629.2068'5—dc22   2007049875

Visit the Taylor & Francis Web site at
http://www.taylorandfrancis.com

and the Productivity Press Web site at
http://www.productivitypress.com

Contents

Foreword

Toyota may well be the most admired and copied company in the world at this moment. A few bad quarters of profits could completely change the high level of interest, but right now that does not seem to be in the cards. It would be hard to find a company that has more consistently had profitable years and grown so steadily over decades. This may from the outside appear to be due to some very clever Japanese tricks, such as just-in-time (JIT) systems to keep inventory low and an overall production and logistics system that continually delivers exceptional quality—but no one inside the company would agree with that analysis. If you were to talk to executives inside the company, you would hear the same theme repeatedly: that their competitive advantage comes from engaging people throughout the enterprise in continuous improvement. Indeed, these days around Toyota, the Toyota Production System (TPS) house has been replaced by the "Toyota Way" house that was presented in *The Toyota Way 2001* by then-president Fujio Cho.

TPS is represented by two pillars—JIT and jidoka. Jidoka refers to equipment with the intelligence to stop itself. Within Toyota, both pillars have to do with problem solving. JIT is a system with very little inventory; problems will shut down the line and cause a sense of urgency to solve them. Jidoka is about equipment and people shutting down the line when there is a problem. Why would you want to shut down the line? The answer is that Toyota leaders do not want to shut down the line as it is costly and can lead to delays in customer shipments. They want to surface problems so that people working in the process will solve those problems at the root cause, thereby making the process stronger. Through this continual strengthening of processes throughout the company all over the world, Toyota becomes a little better every day. Competitors can imitate various tools and methods of JIT and jidoka, but unless they are getting a little better every day for decades, they will not be able to compete with Toyota.

The Toyota way has two different pillars—*respect for people* and *continuous improvement*. The TPS house highlighted technical systems, such as JIT, while this newer version highlights people solving problems. In reality, from the time Taiichi Ohno began developing it, TPS was always about people solving problems—but it was not as explicit in that model. In addition to having more of an explicit focus on the human side, this new model—the Toyota way—is also generic and can be applied to every part of Toyota, not just manufacturing.

The problem-solving method taught to people throughout Toyota, which acts as the toolkit for continuous improvement, is based on what Toyota learned from quality guru W. Edwards Deming decades ago—Plan, Do, Check, Act (PDCA). It has become engrained as an intimate part of the corporate culture. Also engrained in the culture is a way to report on the results of PDCA and that is now becoming well known as the A3 report. The A3 is an 11 x 17-inch piece of paper and the rules of the game are to put the whole report on one side of one sheet. Originally, as it was explained to me, this was the biggest size paper that could fit in a fax machine. I also have witnessed Americans working for Toyota who were struggling to fit their A3 report on A4-sized paper, explaining that Toyota wants even shorter reports written on 8½ x 11-inch paper.

It sort of makes sense that a company so passionate about streamlining its manufacturing plants and squeezing out every drop of waste would strive for a waste-free report. Actually, one of the reasons for such lean processes in Japan was the lack of space and the lack of money when Toyota Motor Company started up. There was no room for extra inventory or the money for the huge pieces of equipment to build large batches. One side of one piece of paper is not a lot of space and one cannot afford non-value-added verbiage in such a small space. In fact, if a picture is worth a thousand words, it makes sense to use pictures when possible on your A3.

I have had the experience more than once of getting a phone call something like the following: "My boss wants to get lean in office operations. We did lean on the shop floor with great success and to take it to the office we need a different tool. He heard something about these A3 reports as a lean tool and ordered me to check it out. He wants all reports to him in the future to be A3 reports." With this type of orientation, there is certainly the risk of A3 reports becoming the office analogue to the kanban[1] card in the factory. There used to be a fad of moving to kanban to eliminate inventory. Print enough cards, make them colorful, seal them up, and you have a pull system just like Toyota. Make kanban electronic and you have passed Toyota. Now, the theory goes, in the office you can write lots of A3 reports and be lean like Toyota. Unfortunately it is not that simple.

This book is aptly entitled *Understanding A3 Thinking: A Critical Component of Toyota's PDCA Management System*. There is a lot hidden in this title. First, you have to understand that A3 is more of a way of thinking than a report-writing methodology. When Toyota went from A3-sized paper to A4-sized paper, they were not fundamentally changing the process. In fact, if they were to suddenly decide you can use both sides of the paper, it would not be an important change. What is important is the underlying philosophy of the methodology.

Second, the philosophy is rooted in the PDCA way of thinking. PDCA is a practical tool for continuous improvement. It is practical in that it provides a framework for action, but practical does not mean easy. PDCA is anything but easy. It is easy to do, do, do. It is very difficult to take the time to really think through the problem and get to the root cause is the plan. It seems even more difficult to check that such changes are really working after the countermeasure is implemented and seems to work, and then to identify further actions to continue improving. Continuous improvement is just that—continuous. You do not solve problems and assume the process is fixed and can be ignored until it breaks down again. Every new stage makes the process a little bit stronger and more robust, but there is always more waste and more room for improvement and conditions will change. So it really is about PDCAPDCAPDCA....

There is a lot to Toyota's problem-solving methodology and the way Toyota engages people in problem solving. Fortunately, we have an A-team who wrote this book and understand the thinking way very deeply. Art Smalley worked for Toyota for many years and was one of a small number of Americans who learned Japanese and worked for Toyota in Japan. After leaving Toyota, he has taken his experience with TPS to many manufacturing companies, continually deepening his understanding in the process. Durward Sobek is a former student of mine and we originally funded him to study Toyota's product development system—but there was a little catch. He had to learn Japanese first and do his research in Japan. He was an A student in accelerated Japanese and went to Japan doing interviews in Japanese. Durward learned how A3 reporting and the underlying PDCA philosophy were the backbone of Toyota's product development system. Between these two men, they understand A3 thinking deeply and have seen many applications in different contexts.

These authors have put together a practical guide filled with excellent examples to teach you how to develop an A3 report. But if you only learn the mechanics, you will be missing the true message of the book. The deeper message is in the thinking process. The A3 provides a disciplined way of reporting on problems that encourages a disciplined way of solving problems. Unfortunately, it is not foolproof, and a poor problem-solving process does not become good because it is documented in a colorful A3. I recommend that you study this book and reflect on the deeper meaning of PDCA. Use the A3 reports as a way of exercising your PDCA abilities and become a student of continuous improvement...throughout your life.

Jeffrey K. Liker

Professor, Industrial and Operations Engineering
University of Michigan

Endnotes

1 A signalling device which gives authorization and instructions for the production or withdrawl of items in a production process.

Acknowledgments

We would like to first thank the good people at Toyota Motor Corporation, who have shared their wisdom with us over the years and continue to be sources of inspiration and insight. Although an exhaustive list of all those who have impacted our thinking on this topic would be too long to list, we would be remiss not to mention the input of Isao Kato, the retired manager of education and training. Toyota managers Tomoo Harada, Mitsuru Kawai, and Mihaya Hayamizu are especially noted for the career and personal developmental of former employee Art Smalley while at Toyota. In addition, numerous people at the Toyota Technical Center were very generous in sharing how they have attempted to translate the practice of A3 reports from Japan to the United States within Toyota's engineering organization—special thanks go to Mike Masaki, Bruce Brownlee, Mary Cassar, and Kris Marvin.

We would also like to thank a number of others who helped make this book a reality: to the late Allen Ward, who gave us the term "A3 thinking"; to Brian and Michael Kennedy, who pushed us to take the subject to a new level and formalize the thinking and processes behind A3 reports; to Cindy Jimmerson, for many wonderful conversations over A3s in-the-making and for sharing her practical insights in implementing the tool real-time in a hospital environment; to Manimay Ghosh, who helped gather A3 examples and whose research gave us additional insight into why the elements of the A3 process work as they do; to Michael Balle, Bill Farmer, Dan Jones, and Katherine Radeka, who reviewed an early draft and provided valuable feedback. We also extend a heartfelt thanks to the editorial staff at Productivity Press for their excellent work in improving the readability of the text.

Funding for this work was provided in part by the National Science Foundation, award #011535. We also thank Montana State University for the time and resources provided to complete the project. Any opinions, findings, conclusions, or recommendations expressed in this material are those of the authors and do not necessarily reflect the views of the National Science Foundation or Montana State University.

Finally, we thank our wives, Sarah and Miwa, and our families and clients. Without their support, none of this work would have been possible.

Introduction

Most modern organizations strive to steadily improve their performance. At a basic level, continuous improvement requires effective problem solving. Unfortunately, we have found that most organizations are not consistently effective in addressing the day-to-day, year-in-and-year-out problems they face. Yes, many have developed sophisticated skills in "fire fighting," but addressing organizational problems to the level that the likelihood of recurrence is greatly diminished remains a rare skill.

In this book, we introduce a general-purpose tool that can greatly improve the problem-solving capabilities of an organization and its members by guiding you through a thorough and candid investigation of your workplace's current issues, encouraging collaboration among organizational members, and concisely documenting decisions, plans, and results. It is general enough to be applied to broad classes of organizational problems; it has been proven effective in a multitude of contexts. And it is conceptually simple—no sophisticated mathematical or technical training is required other than paper, pencil, and basic literacy.

The tool is called the A3 report, after the size of paper that has traditionally been used. What we describe in these pages was developed by Toyota; it is based on our research and experience with Toyota professionals over many years, along with our own experiences using the tool in U.S. organizations. Other companies have used similar tools with good effect. However, in all cases, the tools are effective only to the extent they engender a style of thinking that is rigorous and thorough, a style of communication that focuses on hard data and vital information, and a style of problem solving that is collaborative and objective. Thus the title of this book attempts to emphasize that the processes used to develop the documents are as important as—or more important than—the documents themselves.

To comprehend the power of A3 reports and the thinking behind them requires a good grasp of the Plan-Do-Check-Act (PDCA) cycle. PDCA is a high-level methodology for continuous improvement that has long been a basic element of the Total Quality Management movement. As we explain in chapter

1, PDCA is the basic philosophy behind A3 thinking. Unfortunately, we have found that many managers are not familiar with PDCA, and many of those who are familiar do not really understand it. So we devote the better part of the first chapter explaining PDCA and its fundamental importance.

A3 thinking is as much about developing good problem-solvers as it is about effectively solving problems. Thus, chapter 2 focuses on understanding the methods that problem-solvers use and that the system is designed to develop. We articulate seven elements of A3 thinking—that is, the kind of thinking that the A3 report tool encourages—and the A3 process that add some meat to the PDCA skeleton, making it more actionable and useful.

At the same time, we outline a practical set of tools that, together with an understanding of the system and its logic, can be implemented quickly and with good effect. Chapter 3 describes the most basic form of A3 report: the problem-solving A3. Chapters 4 and 5 detail two other common forms of A3 reports: the proposal A3 and the status A3. Each general type of report is useful for specific situations; these chapters describe the general outline of the reports with examples and templates, and provide exercises to give the reader an opportunity to learn by doing. Each chapter also has a section on reviewing A3 reports. The review system plays a central role in the system, as it is the primary mechanism to ensure that rigorous processes are followed. It also represents a key mechanism within Toyota for mentoring individuals in solving problems.

Following these chapters, we then take a chapter to outline a few of the mechanics of writing A3 reports that are applicable regardless of type. The focus is on style and form as opposed to the content focus of prior chapters. Then we devote chapter 7 to questions about support structures that will be helpful to designing and implementing an A3 report system that will be effective on an organization-wide basis. The issues discussed here are not critical to getting started, but they will gain importance as the system grows and is put into practice throughout the organization. The conclusion (chapter 8) offers some final thoughts on moving forward, drawing largely from our experiences implementing the system in American organizations.

The description of the PDCA management system described herein is based on our observation and the research of Toyota and, in the case of the second author, personal experience writing A3 reports under Toyota mentorship. We are indebted to Toyota for the opportunities to understand its system and can take little credit for most of the ideas, as we learned almost everything from the fine people at Toyota. However, even though the system grew out of automotive manufacturing, it is broadly applicable to almost any management system. In fact, internally, Toyota uses the system in manufacturing, production engineering, product development, sales, marketing, and even in the executive ranks. Such a broad spectrum of applicability suggests that this system is transportable to many sectors. In fact, the first author has successfully applied the system in a health-care context with excellent results.

So we invite you on a journey, one in which you will understand how to approach organizational problems and capitalize on new opportunities, practically and effectively, as the backbone of your continuous improvement endeavors. Even if the full system is not adopted by your organization (although we sincerely hope it will be), you can dramatically improve your personal effectiveness by applying the processes, thinking, and tools described in the following pages. So come, explore, and most importantly, put what you learn from these pages into practice.

Chapter 1

A Basis for Managerial Effectiveness

Toyota Motor Corporation is arguably the most studied company of the modern era. More than a dozen books[1] have been written about the company, its management system and philosophy, and its approaches to various business and operational problems. One of the latest books, *The Toyota Way* by Jeffrey Liker[2], became an immediate best-seller, indicating the instant draw the Toyota name has within the business community. A search on Business Source Premier (http://www.uwe.ac.uk) turned up over 3,000 articles published over a ten-year period with "Toyota" in the title. And this number does not include the hundreds of volumes and countless articles on lean manufacturing or various aspects thereof (for example, 5S, kanban, poka-yoke) that are largely based on tools and practices developed by Toyota.

Such attention is well deserved. As of the writing of this book, Toyota had just surpassed Ford Motor Company in number of vehicles sold annually in the United States, having already beat out Ford in global sales several years prior, and it is poised to topple General Motors to become the largest auto manufacturer in the world. In 2005, Toyota produced one vehicle approximately every four seconds somewhere in the world while at the same time setting the benchmark for product quality. Toyota perennially wins national and international acclaim in all of the major automobile-quality ratings. For instance, Toyota's flagship Lexus nameplate has earned the top spot in J. D. Power's Initial Quality Survey for over ten years running. On top of all this, Toyota is profitable—in fact, very profitable. Toyota set record profits in 2003, 2004, and 2005, earning over $10 billion annually, even while its North American competitors saw significant drops in earnings, and even losses.

But other companies have also been successful. What makes Toyota intriguing is that its success has been sustained over an extremely long time period, by most business standards. From the ashes of World War II, Toyota initially struggled to maintain solvency but rose over the following decades to become Japan's leading manufacturer. As it grew, Toyota began seeking markets outside of Japan, and by the early 1980s, Toyota was well established in the U.S. market. Toyota has grown each year for the past fifty years and has not experienced a loss in net earnings since the early 1950s. This is a standout performance in an industry characterized by cyclical ups and downs.

Toyota is also intriguing because its business and management philosophy is unique, its approach to manufacturing is exceptional and counterintuitive, and its collective understanding of operational dynamics is breathtakingly insightful. Toyota is perhaps most well known for its production system, first documented in a detailed eighty-page handbook published internally in Japanese in 1973. The first English publication on it appeared in 1977 by Sugimori et al.[3] as a high-level summary. However, it was not until the early 1990s that the uniqueness of Toyota's system became well known, with the publication of the book *The Machine That Changed the World*.[4] In it, the MIT professors detail the strikingly robust, flexible, and efficient systems they observed in Japan, and dubbed it "lean manufacturing" for their ability to design, produce, and deliver higher-quality products in volume with a fraction of the resources used by their North American and European competitors. The manufacturing community learned later that the model of lean manufacturing was the Toyota Production System (TPS).

Toyota has been remarkably open in sharing its system with others, even establishing the Toyota Supplier Support Center to provide consulting assistance to U.S. companies wanting to operate more efficiently, at no cost to the client. More recently, we have come to understand that Toyota's uniqueness extends into many other areas as well, including product development and logistics. Cottage industries are sprouting in many arenas to provide training in lean tools and concepts and assistance in implementation. Lean applications that were once targeted primarily at high-volume manufacturing plants are rapidly finding their way into other sectors of the economy, including engineering, financial services, transportation and logistics, health care, food and beverage services, and government (including military operations). Toyota's impact is being felt well beyond the automotive industry.

PDCA: Heart of the Toyota Way

The lean model is dramatically altering the face of manufacturing in the developed world. Inventories are dropping, lead times are shortening, quality is holding steady or increasing, and prices are falling. We expect this trend will follow in other sectors, just as it has in manufacturing. Yet, to our knowledge, with all that we know, with all that has been published, with all the resources that are available, no American companies have reached Toyota's level of efficiency and effectiveness. In fact, Toyota is building factories in the United States even as most of U.S. manufacturing is trying to move operations overseas or outsource them altogether. Why do we not see more companies emulating Toyota's success?

While there may be many explanations, perhaps the most crucial one is that most of us do not understand—or if we understand, do not appreciate—what is at the heart of the Toyota business, management, and manufacturing approach. We tend to see the intricate set of tools as the system. But although they are important to the system as currently enacted, they are at the surface, not the heart. In fact, Taiichi Ohno, the father of the modern Toyota production system, said that the tools are just countermeasures to business problems that Toyota has faced and that they will be used only until better countermeasures are found.[5] In other words, the interconnected web of tools and practices we know as lean manufacturing is the outcome of a deeper set of processes. These deeper processes, we argue, are at the heart of Toyota's system.

So how did the Toyota system emerge? In simple terms, it emerged as Toyota's people saw problems or opportunities, "solved" the problems aggressively and systematically to find a better way to do things, and then rigorously verified that the better way was indeed better. If the remedy did indeed improve the system, the new way became the standard way to do the work; if not, problem solving and verification continue until the problem is satisfactorily addressed.

The roots of this process are grounded in the scientific method of inquiry. The founders of the original Toyota companies were Sakichi Toyoda and his son, Kiichiro. Sakichi is recognized in Japanese textbooks as one of the great inventors of his time. His primary accomplishment was the creation of an automatic loom in 1924 that far surpassed the productivity and quality of any similar product on the market at that time. Over 24 patents were granted on this machine alone. Most of the patents were filed by Sakichi; however, quite a few were also developed by his son, Kiichiro, a graduate of the mechanical engineering department of Tokyo University, the most prestigious university in Japan. Like his father, he had a knack for invention and liked to create and tinker by nature. The machines they developed emerged out of repeated experimentation. This inclination toward actions, and of trying out ideas through experimentation, continues to this day.[6]

The problem-solving approaches in use at Toyota today are also deeply influenced by a high-level methodology initially developed by Walter Shewhart of Bell Labs in the 1930s, and later adopted by W. Edwards Deming who became its biggest proselytizer.[7] The methodology is the Plan-Do-Check-Act (PDCA) cycle, also called the Deming Cycle. Additional education came from representatives of the Japan Union of Scientists and Engineers (JUSE), who put on lectures at Toyota and other manufacturing companies in Japan after World War II, teaching scientific principles for quality control and improvement.[8] The heart of these teachings is the PDCA cycle.

The PDCA cycle begins with the Plan step, in which the problem-solver thoroughly studies a problem or opportunity to understand it from as many viewpoints as possible, analyzes it (quantitatively, if possible) to find the root causes, develops one or more ideas to remedy the problem or seize the opportunity, and devises a plan for implementation. In the Do step, the plan is put into action as immediately as is possible and prudent. The Check step involves measuring the effects of implementation and comparing them to the target or prediction. Act refers to establishing the new process, solution, or system as the standard if the results are satisfactory, or taking remedial action if they are not. The PDCA cycle simply follows the steps of the scientific method: Plan is developing a hypothesis and experimental design; Do is conducting the experiment; Check is collecting measurements; and Act is interpreting the results and taking appropriate action.

Over the years, Toyota has honed a set of norms and practices on how to most effectively conduct each step of the cycle. At each juncture, the problem-solver tries to confront his or her own assumptions and preconceptions in order to gain insight into a situation or phenomenon, or to validate that his or her understanding is accurate. If one gains insight, that new learning must be confirmed through experimentation. If one's current understanding is found deficient, immediate remedial action is required.

What Don't We Get?

None of this should sound new or exotic to Western managers. Indeed, the concepts of the scientific method or PDCA are ironically Western and not original to Japanese culture. So why have so many organizations not embraced this process or style of thinking to the extent that Toyota has? We believe multiple reasons exist.

Perhaps most significantly, in the West, we tend to be oriented toward short-term results. We want to get the problem taken care of and move on. At Toyota, however, the process by which the results are achieved is equally—if not more—

important, and the ultimate goal is not just a problem resolved in the immediate term, but also that 1) the problem is less likely to occur in the future because the overall system is improved, and 2) the problem-solver has enhanced his or her problem-solving skills and is prepared to tackle even more challenging tasks in the future. This difference in perspectives fundamentally alters the way we see PDCA.

It has been said that the typical U.S. firm, when facing a vexing problem in which it has one year to solve, would spend three months planning, three months implementing, and six months tweaking and picking up loose ends. Toyota, facing a similar situation, would spend eleven months planning and one month implementing (with no loose ends to clean up!). This comparison is an exaggeration, of course, but it nonetheless contains an important element of truth. The reason Toyota spends so much time and effort on the planning phase is because that phase is so critical to learning. Toyota managers want to make sure they deeply understand the background and facts of the current situation before moving forward. After the current state is thoroughly probed, they want to establish a high degree of certainty that they have accurately identified the root cause of the problem. This includes understanding the situation from multiple perspectives, not just one's own, and gathering and analyzing system performance quantitatively.

Toyota's problem-solvers also plan out the change in detail (including which steps will be taken, by whom, and when) and get consensus from each individual involved and, if appropriate, their supervisors. This level of implementation planning is important to learning because if the expected improvement is not achieved, the team will want to know whether it was lack of understanding of the situation or a faulty implementation that produced the disappointing results.

Furthermore, thorough planning includes a reasonable prediction of the change in performance, along with a plan to follow up—again, who will do what and when. The prediction of future performance is actually an informal statement of hypothesis based on the current state of knowledge. It is the a priori statement of hypothesis (that is, prior to experimentation) that enables learning to occur at the follow-up. We either confirm our current understanding or unequivocally find out that we have more to learn. Without the hypothesis, the scientific method quickly devolves into a guess-and-check or trial-and-error approach, with commensurate declines in learning.

With the planning function complete, the plan can be executed. Simply, the Do step must be accomplished for any change to occur. Although this may seem obvious, many organizations seem content to spend all of their time in meetings and never actually get around to doing anything about the problems identified. Toyota recognizes that the Do step is essential. It is the experiment to test the hypothesis.

The Check step, then, is where the individuals involved validate their current level of understanding, a vital step of the learning process. How do we know that what we think we learned and understood in the Plan step is actually accurate? Toyota does this by following Shewhart's and Deming's advice and measuring the actual results. If actual results correspond to those predicted, the problem-solving team confirms that what they thought they understood is probably accurate. In other words, the knowledge has been validated. If actual results do not match the predicted outcome, more investigation is needed to find out why. The team will also want to make sure the implementation plan took place as planned (if not, of course, then why not).

Finally, the Act step identifies any loose ends or modifications to be made based on the learning from the Check cycle. It is also the step where the change becomes institutionalized for improved system performance and learning is shared with appropriate parts of the organization. It would seem obvious that we would not want to institutionalize a change until we verify that the organization will actually perform better as a result; however, many organizations routinely institute system changes without a clear idea of the effects the change will have.

Thus we see that while many managers have heard of PDCA, most do not understand that it involves more than just getting problems resolved in a timely fashion. PDCA is a high-level methodology to raise both individual and organizational consciousness about what is known and what is not known in order to resolve the problems currently faced and to prevent future recurrence. At the same time, PDCA aims to improve long-term system performance, not just take care of a localized problem. As the preceding discussion demonstrates, to use the cycle effectively requires a certain level of discipline.

A short story might help illustrate the point. While one of the authors was a young trainee in Japan, he was asked to solve a quality problem on a precision grinding machine. Initially, he proposed changing several parameters all at once to "fix" the problem. Instead, his supervisor had him sketch the machine in considerable detail and make a Pareto chart of all the different types of defects on the machine. This exercise isolated one particular type of defect as the main cause for concern. The supervisor then had the trainee list all the potential causes of the defect one by one using a fishbone diagram.

Because a positive cause-and-effect relationship could not be established by deduction alone, the trainee was required to come up with a list of corrective actions to attempt for each potential cause. He tested them one by one. Finally, after several days, he had a breakthrough when the coolant lubricating the part during the grinding cycle was analyzed and subsequently changed out. Bacteria had contaminated the coolant. After replacing the coolant, defects dropped from 2.3% to under 0.2%.

The trainee proudly reported the good news to his supervisor and the manager of production. Expecting words of praise, he was somewhat chagrined when they did not seem entirely pleased. The trainee was told essentially, "Thank you for your efforts. By the way, have you considered how the coolant managed to get contaminated in the first place? What checks do we have in place to sample coolant for this problem? Who is in charge of the coolant check process? How can we prevent coolant contamination in the future?"

The words and questions were not harsh or overly negative. They were framed with a specific purpose in mind. Yes, solving this local problem on one machine was nice. However, development of the trainee's ability to solve problems and see the larger issues was more important. Furthermore, a breakthrough is worthy of accolades only when true cause-and-effect relationships are established and true countermeasures (i.e., how to stop coolant contamination from occurring, in this case) are put into effect that will prevent recurrence of the problem. This not-so-subtle distinction is the difference between merely good problem-solvers and outstanding ones.

A System to Support PDCA Management

We argue that Toyota's attention-getting success stems more fundamentally from a management philosophy and culture that is firmly grounded in PDCA than from the mere use of lean tools. Unlike some elements of Toyota's approach that authors have claimed is innate and unspoken (and therefore difficult to elicit because Toyota people are not conscious of it), this element is quite explicit and ubiquitous throughout Toyota. In staff meetings, in one-on-one mentoring, in internal training manuals and courses, and even in public presentations, PDCA is mentioned explicitly as an overriding philosophy in nearly everything Toyota undertakes. We further argue that failure to fully appreciate the details and rigor of the PDCA role means that one will have difficulty understanding Toyota beyond its tools and practices, and as such will likely never achieve the promise of lean.

Our purpose in writing this book, however, is not to focus on PDCA as a general management approach, although we have started out this way because it is an essential backdrop to the ideas expressed on the following pages. Nor is our aim to explain Toyota, though we will do some of that as well. Rather, our purpose is to outline a simple system for implementing PDCA management—a system that is simple yet disciplined and rigorous. It centers on the use of what Toyota terms A3 reports, one-page documents that record the main results from the PDCA cycle. (A3 reports are so named because they fit on one side of an A3-sized sheet of paper, which is roughly equivalent to an 11 x 17-inch sheet.) The report templates serve as guidelines for addressing the root causes of problems that arise in and around the workplace in a rigorous and systematic way. The reports that emerge from the process document the plans so that they can be discussed, scrutinized, and once approved, followed. They further invite reflection and introspection on what learning has taken place and document that learning for future reference. And they create a focal point for coaching and mentoring.

Although the reports are the centerpiece of the system, the documents are not, on their own, the system. Toyota's system, as we've come to understand it, includes processes for approaching and following up on problems and opportunities, and it is the processes, more so than the documents, that lead to the results. Merely completing an A3 report will do little for the organization in the absence of an appropriate process. Furthermore, we want you, the reader, to understand the thinking behind the system, as the title of the book implies. Not all problems or opportunities at Toyota are addressed using an A3 report; however, the thought processes behind the system are nearly always invoked, and it is this that we want to elucidate. Furthermore, the style of thinking in the reports is not merely deployed in the manufacturing departments of the company—it is used in every function of the company at every level. Let us now take a detailed look at what we call A3 thinking.

Endnotes

1 For example, M. A. Cusumano, *The Japanese Automobile Industry: Technology and Management at Nissan and Toyota* (Cambridge, MA: Council on East Asian Studies and Harvard University, 1986); T. Ohno, *Toyota Production System: Beyond Large-Scale Production* (Cambridge, MA: Productivity Press, 1988); S. Shingo, *A Study of the Toyota Production System from an Industrial Engineering Viewpoint* (Cambridge, MA: Productivity Press, 1989); Japan Management Association and D. J. Lu, Kanban *Just-in-Time at Toyota: Management Begins at the Workplace* (Cambridge, MA: Productivity Press, 1989); Y. Monden, *The Toyota Management System: Linking the Seven Key Functional Areas* (Cambridge, MA: Productivity Press, 1996); T. L. Besser, *Team Toyota: Transplanting the Toyota Culture to the Camry Plant in Kentucky* (Albany, NY: SUNY Press, 1996); M. A. Cusumano and N. Kentaro, *Thinking beyond Lean: How Multi-Project Management Is Transforming Product Development at Toyota* (New York: Free Press, 1998); Y. Monden, *Toyota Production System: An Integrated Approach to Just-in-Time* (Norcross, GA: Engineering & Management Press, 1998); T. Fujimoto, *The Evolution of a Manufacturing System at Toyota* (New York: Oxford University Press, 1999); M. N. Kennedy, *Product Development for the Lean Enterprise: Why Toyota's System Is Four Times More Productive*, Richmond VA: The Oaklea Press 2003; S. Hino, *Inside the*

Mind of Toyota: Management Principles for Enduring Growth (New York: Productivity Press, 2005); J. M. Morgan and J. K. Liker, *The Toyota Product Development System: Integrating People, Process and Technology* (New York: Productivity Press, 2006).

2 J. K. Liker, *The Toyota Way: 14 Management Principles from the World's Greatest Manufacturer* (New York: McGraw-Hill, 2005).

3 Y. Sugimori, K. Kusunoki, F. Cho, and S. Uchikawa (1977) "Toyota Production System and Kanban System: Materialization of Just-in-Time and Respect-for-Human System," *International Journal of Production Research*, 15(6): 553–64.

4 J. P. Womack, D. T. Jones, and D. Roos, *The Machine That Changed the World* (New York: HarperPerennial, 1990).

5 Ohno is credited as the architect of what we know as lean manufacturing, including the concepts of just-in-time, kanban, and one-piece or continuous flow. See T. Ohno, *Toyota Production System: Beyond Large-Scale Production* (Portland, OR: Productivity Press, 1988).

6 Wada Kazuo and Yui Tsunehiko, *Kiichiro Den: The Life of Kiichiro Toyoda* (Nagoya, Japan: Nagoya University Publishing, 2002). © Toyota Motor Corporation, 2002.

7 W. A. Shewhart, *Statistical Method from the Viewpoint of Quality Control* (New York: Dover, 1939); HCi, "PDCA Cycle," www.hci.com.au/hcisite3/toolkit/pdcacycl.htm (accessed December 2007).

8 Andrea Gabor, *The Man Who Discovered Quality* (New York: Times Books, 1990).

Chapter 2

A3 Thinking

The A3 report is a powerful tool. It establishes a concrete structure to implement PDCA management. It helps draw the report author(s) to a deeper understanding of the problem or opportunity, and it gives insight into how to address that problem. It facilitates cohesion and alignment within the organization as to the best course of action. But as with any tool, one must know how to use an A3 report. As mentioned in the introduction, the tool itself is less important than the thinking promoted by using it. Therefore, without the broader picture in mind, even strict adherence to the guidelines for A3 report writing presented in later chapters would miss the point, resulting in adherents who value form over substance.

To avoid this situation, we describe in this chapter the kind of thinking that an A3 report system promotes. We believe—and trust you will agree—that the kind of thinking we are talking about is actually quite rare in most organizations and yet creates a tremendously capable workforce. That increased workforce capability translates into highly effective and continuously improving work systems and outstanding organizational performance. A3 thinking, we believe, is the key to avoiding form over substance when using A3 reports.

In addition, A3 reports cannot be drafted in isolation by someone working exclusively in his or her cubicle. There is a process of sorts—a set of principles enacted in rough sequence—that calls out a set of behaviors needed to leverage the power of the A3 report as a collaborative problem-solving tool. So the second half of this chapter describes a practical approach to problem solving that is derived from our work on Toyota.

Viewing problem solving as primarily a cerebral activity would be inconsistent with the PDCA philosophy, with A3 thinking, and with the Toyota way.

Specific actions are needed to precipitate the right modes of thinking, which lead to the next actions and even deeper thinking, and so forth, in a never-ending cycle of thinking and acting to produce the desired improvements. Thus we present these two sides together—the thinking and the behaviors—in one chapter to convey this essential point.

Seven Elements of A3 Thinking

As we reflect on our experiences and research of Toyota, we find that intellectual development of people is a high priority at Toyota. We also find that Toyota uses the A3 report system as a way to cultivate the intellectual development of its members, and the company management intentionally attempts to steer that development in specific ways. We have distilled the mind-set behind the A3 system to seven elements:

1. Logical thinking process
2. Objectivity
3. Results and process
4. Synthesis, distillation, and visualization
5. Alignment
6. Coherence within and consistency across
7. Systems viewpoint

Let us look at each of these elements in turn, and see how A3 thinking is the basis for effective, real-time problem solving.

Element 1: Logical Thinking Process

Perhaps more than anything else, Toyota wants its people to be able to think and then act rationally in decision making and problem solving. The basic structure and technique embodied in A3 report writing is a combination of discipline when executing PDCA mixed with a heavy dose of the scientific method of investigation. Reflecting upon his time at Toyota, one of the authors is amazed at the emphasis and importance placed upon factually discerning the difference between "cause" and "effect" in the daily world of production. Conversely, Toyota views the inability to properly discern between cause and effect as the leading cause of many poor decisions and problems that remain unsolved in daily management.

As many Toyota managers are fond of saying, the unfortunate reality is that organizations face an infinite number of problems to solve but have only a finite amount of resources available to tackle them. Successful companies like Toyota are able to develop people to recognize the most important problems facing a business or a process (for example, 80/20 rule insights[1]), and instill in the employee the obligation and capability to solve the problems expeditiously.

The benefits are not only tactical in terms of generating results; A3 thinking is also tremendously powerful because it creates consistent, socially constructed approaches to key classes of problems, so that members within the organization spend less time spinning their wheels or trying to figure out how another person is approaching a given situation. This is an important but often overlooked dynamic about Toyota Motor Corporation. They simply have less waste of management time through more focused and productive meetings, and less attention devoted to the wrong things.

Properly utilized A3 reports, and the underlying thinking patterns, help to promote and reinforce logical thought processes that are thorough and address all important details, consider numerous potential avenues, take into account the effects of implementation, anticipate possible stumbling blocks, and incorporate contingencies. The processes apply to issues of goal setting, policymaking, and daily decision making just as much as they do to business, organizational, and engineering problem solving.

Element 2: Objectivity

Because human observation is inherently subjective, every person sees the world a little bit differently. As such, the mental representations of the reality people experience can be quite different, and each tends to believe his or her representation is the "right" one. In most cases, individuals within an organization have enough common understanding that they can communicate and work together to get things done. But quite often, when they get into the details of the situation, the common understanding starts to break down, and the differences in how we see reality become apparent.

As an illustrative example, consider a machine-intensive shop experiencing a lot of mechanical downtime on equipment.[2] Everyone in the shop knows that equipment downtime is the problem. However, agreement on what to do is another matter. Production blames maintenance for slow response time, inadequate skill, or lack of urgency. Maintenance in turn blames production for not doing daily cleaning of the machines, for not giving them time to do preventive maintenance, or for failing to communicate the problem symptoms early enough. Both sides have a highly subjective and emotional viewpoint regarding the situation, which puts blinders on both their objectivity and their logical thinking. The natural reaction, if a person feels his or her representation is right, is to view the other's as "wrong." This can quickly devolve into the blame game that is so common in situations involving cross-departmental participation.

A3 thinking, on the other hand, attempts to reconcile those multiple viewpoints, in part because a view of the situation that includes multiple perspectives tends to be more objective than any single viewpoint. The problem-solvers necessarily start with their own picture of the situation and make it explicit so that they can better share it with others and test it. They collect quantitative (that is, objective) facts and discuss their picture with others to verify that the picture is accurate. If it is not, they make the appropriate adjustments until it is an accurate representation of, as some would argue, a co-constructed reality. In other words, it is a co-constructed representation of a co-constructed reality.

Returning to the maintenance-versus-production debate, it would be more useful to learn that, of the 120 machines in the plant, just seven were causing most of the downtime, and that, upon further investigation, five of the machines were out of service for extended periods due to lack of mechanical spare parts. The parts were on order but stuck in purchasing due to incorrect vendor information in the order form. The problem is still serious, but the discussion on what to do about it is entirely different. In this example, neither the skill nor the motivation of production employees or maintenance technicians was the root cause of the issue. And the problem will repeat in the future unless the framing of the problem changes.

The point is, objectivity is a central component to the A3 thinking mind-set. Effective problem-solvers continually test their understanding of a situation for assumptions, biases, and misconceptions. The process begins by framing the problem with relevant facts and details, as objectively as possible. Furthermore, suggested remedies or recommended courses of action should promote the organizational good, not (even if subconsciously) personal agendas. There is little room in A3 thinking for qualitative opinion or wishful thinking.

Element 3: Results and Process

For all the attention placed upon Toyota for its vaunted production process, it is actually a very results-oriented organization. Aggressive business and operational goals are set, and both individuals and teams are evaluated based on how well they achieve those goals. But at Toyota, achieving goals using sloppy processes is not acceptable. The ends simply do not justify the means. Our colleague John Shook, who worked for Toyota in Japan, frequently comments, "It is important to obtain results in Toyota but also to obtain them following the correct way"—that is, the Toyota way. A3 thinking is as much about personal development as it is about achieving results, so the processes used become paramount. Toyota mentors want to know clearly and specifically how well a person understands the problem, investigates alternatives, knows how the proposal fits into the larger picture, and so forth, so that the results test one's understanding.

Achieving results accidentally or by happenstance is of little long-term value. With an A3 approach, the process can be refined and repeated for better results in the future.

At the same time, following the process and not achieving results is equally ineffective. The results truly are a test of one's understanding. Poor results not only fail to move the organization forward but also reflect a poor understanding, a situation that simply must be rectified. So we continue to apply the process (that is, apply PDCA) until we achieve results that reflect an acceptable level of understanding.

Take the example of an insurance company that handles many requests for quotes submitted from field agents. The turnaround time for an average quote is five days. The problem is that, by the time the quote gets back to the field agent, the client is often lost to a competing company. To remedy the situation, management could hire more people to process the quotes more quickly or could pressure employees to work harder or faster. These approaches may indeed produce results; however, in Toyota's way of thinking, they are not acceptable. Toyota management would want to know the reason for the five-day turnaround time. Is it missing information? Is it poor flow in processing the quote? Is the approval process too lengthy? Do employees lack the right level of training? To Toyota, figuring out the real root cause and then solving that issue to shorten the turnaround time to one day or less with existing resources is the "right" process to use. A process that quickly jumps to a solution (as in, hiring more analysts) without a good grasp of the root causes, though it may achieve the desired results, would not be viewed as a successful project.

Thus the third element of A3 thinking says that both results and process are important. Results are not favored over the process used to achieve them, nor is process elevated above results. Both are necessary and critical to effective organizational improvement and personnel development.

Element 4: Synthesis, Distillation, and Visualization

A3 reports are brief, by design. Many American managers we have spoken with about the A3 concept are enamored with this characteristic—they have read too many reports where the critical piece of information is hidden in a footnote twenty pages in, or witnessed too many PowerPoint presentations where the key insight appears as the fourth bullet on slide 56. A brief report that hits the main point directly would be a breath of fresh air. However, brevity for brevity's sake is not the point, although it is an attractive side benefit.

The point of the brevity is to force synthesis of the learning acquired in the course of researching the problem or opportunity and discussing it with others. The exercise causes multiple pieces of information from different sources to be integrated into a coherent picture of the situation and recommended future action. Furthermore, not all the information obtained is equally salient. So the report author must distill the synthesized picture to only the most vital points needed for proper positioning and understanding.

Toyota managers and executives like to have face time with all employees and team members. In a pyramid-style organization such as Toyota's with over 200,000 employees worldwide, this becomes difficult at higher levels of the company. Frequently, however, the president and other members of the executive ranks visit the shop floor. When they do, simple flip charts or single-page A3 reports are used for brief presentations about the status of work in an area of problem solving. These presentations almost always follow a fairly standard format—what we call A3 thinking—that can provide an amazing amount of detail along with employee narration. Time spent sorting through repetitive and often confusing verbal explanations is eliminated, allowing the executive or manager to interact with more groups on a highly productive basis.

Very often, the most efficient way to convey information is through a graphical representation. As an industrial engineering professor, the first author has read many student reports that ramble on for pages describing a process or work system, when a simple graphic could convey the same information more quickly in less space. Similarly, a simple sketch of the process and problem can eliminate a thousand words and the associated explanation time and energy required. Thus A3 thinking encourages the visualization of the key synthesized information in order to communicate the message clearly and efficiently. Indeed, in many cases, the act of creating the visualization aids the synthesis and distillation process.

Element 5: Alignment

Many authors argue that effective implementation of a change often hinges on obtaining prior consensus among the parties involved. With consensus, everyone pulls together to overcome obstacles and make the change happen. Similarly, the fifth element of A3 thinking highlights the high value Toyota places on developing agreement around decisions to take specific courses of action. Putting the key facts of the situation, the thinking process, the proposed action, and the follow-up plan in writing gives each person affected something concrete to which he or she can agree or disagree.

Alignment in A3 thinking typically involves 3D communication: horizontally across the organization, up and down the hierarchy, and back and forth in time. The problem-solving team communicates horizontally with other groups in the organization possibly affected by the proposed change and incorporates their concerns into the solution. The team also communicates vertically with individuals who are on the front lines (say, first-level engineers) to see how they may be affected, and with managers up the hierarchy to determine whether any broader issues have not been addressed. Finally, it is important that the history of the situation be taken into account, including past remedies, and that recommendations for action consider possible exigencies that may occur in the future. Taking all these into consideration will result in mutually agreeable, innovative recommendations. Furthermore, the fact that A3 reports are written means they can be referred to at a future date, helping ensure that follow-up and evaluation are consistent and aligned with the original plan.

Toyota, like many Japanese organizations, places a high value on consensus, but it is a practical consensus. Toyota recognizes that 100 percent consensus will not be possible in all cases, so in cases where problem-solvers are not able to incorporate a person's concerns, they are expected to return to that person and explain why those concerns were not addressed. The purpose of this conversation is more than just a courtesy. It is a tangible act to show that the concerns were taken seriously, and it is an implicit request for the individual to sacrifice some of his or her interests for the greater good. Both foster alignment of the organization.

Element 6: Coherency Within and Consistency Across

One of the key points in writing A3 reports is to establish a logical flow from one section of the report to the next. This promotes coherency within the problem-solving approach, part of the sixth element of A3 thinking.

We often see problem-solving efforts that are ineffective simply because the problem-solvers do not maintain coherency. They tackle problems that are not important to the organization's goals, propose solutions that do not address the root causes, or even outline implementation plans that leave out key pieces of the proposed solution. So coherency within the problem-solving approach is paramount to effective problem resolution.

Use of A3 reports reinforces a generalized pattern of problem solving and makes the coherency of one's approach (or lack thereof) visible. In drafting an A3 report, the theme or issue should be consistent with the organization's goals and values. The diagnosis of the present situation falls in line with the theme. The root-cause analysis follows directly from the analysis of the current situation. The proposed remedies address the root causes identified. The implementation plan puts the remedies into place. The follow-up plan tests the results of the remedies against the targets established earlier in the report.

At the same time, because the flow of different A3 types (designated for different organizational situations) is common across Toyota, the organization is able to establish a high level of consistency across organizational units. Consistent approaches speed up communication and aid in establishing shared understanding. Organizational members understand the implicit logic of the approach, so they can anticipate and offer information that will be helpful to the problem-solvers as they move through the process.

Element 7: Systems Viewpoint

Maintaining a systems viewpoint is a strong value at Toyota, and is reflected in the seventh and final element of A3 thinking. Before one engages in a specific course of action, the individual is mentored to develop a deep understanding of:

- The purpose of the course of action;
- How the course of action furthers the organization's goals, needs, and priorities; and
- How it fits into the larger picture and affects other parts of the organization.

A solution that solves a problem in one part of the organization only to create another one in some other part of the organization is generally avoided. Similarly, a recommendation to pursue a course of action that promotes one organizational goal at the expense of all others is also unlikely to receive a favorable hearing. The point is, the problem-solver should understand the situation in a sufficiently broad context, and a recommendation should promote the overall good of the organization.

Universities often suffer from not taking a systems viewpoint when facing challenges. For example, if an academic program finds that students are not getting sufficient background in a given area, a common solution is to add a course on that topic. But doing so increases instructional load, taking teaching resources that could be used for other things, such as graduate student support or research, and also increases student burden. In essence, one goal is furthered, but others are hindered. In the manufacturing world, production departments can always make more units on any given day to superficially improve productivity measures. However, this can result in overproduction, one of the seven wastes of the Toyota Production System (TPS), if making more does not translate into more sales dollars or impact bottom-line profits. An individual department's numbers may look good, but overall organization performance stays the same or becomes worse, suggesting that a systems viewpoint is absent.

In summary, although we have presented the elements of A3 thinking as seven distinct pieces, they, in fact, interact and reinforce each other. Most of the elements, for example, can be seen as extensions of the systems viewpoint or logical thinking processes. We would argue that if you want logical thinkers in your organization who take a systems approach to the problems they encounter, you would do well to promote objectivity, encourage synthesis and distillation of the most relevant information, diligently seek organizational alignment (at the appropriate levels) for recommended courses of action, maintain consistency across organizational units in organizational approach and coherence within any given problem-solving instance, and evaluate performance based on both process and results.

Practical Problem Solving

The elements of A3 thinking form a critical backdrop in understanding how and why the A3 tool works, but these elements are not necessarily very actionable. Merely saying, "Let's take a systems viewpoint" is generally insufficient to accomplishing anything real toward that end. So we turn the discussion now to specific actions that promote the kind of thinking described in the preceding sections. Writing A3 reports is important but not nearly as important as the activities executed in the creation of the report and the conversations that the reports help generate. In fact, in Toyota's internal training program, students cannot take a course in A3 report writing until they have completed the PDCA management course and a course on practical problem solving. We have described the main elements of PDCA management in chapter 1. We now do the same for practical problem solving.

We have distilled a general process for approaching problems that occur during the course of work, based on our observations and research on Toyota (see figure 2.1). The same basic process is followed for proposals to take advantage of opportunities. The process appears serial, but in fact it tends to be iterative in nature, as steps are repeated as needed to remedy any shortcomings or address concerns that arise at a later stage. Also, the steps may not occur strictly in the order presented, although generally speaking, loop backs aside, the general flow holds. The first seven steps represent the Plan step of the PDCA cycle. After approval, the team immediately enters the Do step, followed by the Check step. If results are satisfactory, the new change becomes standard operating procedure, completing the Act step of PDCA; otherwise, the whole process begins anew, as indicated by the dashed loop-back arrow. We will now discuss each step at some length.

Grasping the Current Situation

The problem-solving step that perhaps most distinguishes Toyota from any other company is the first step of the problem-solving cycle: grasping the current situation. What Toyota means by this phrase is gaining a thorough understanding of the process or system that gave rise to the problem, in the context where the problem occurred. The context is critical because, frequently, the key to resolv-

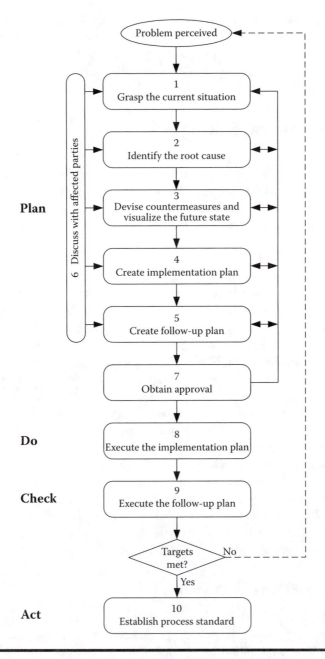

Figure 2.1 Practical problem-solving process

ing a problem is in a detail that no one has yet noticed (for if anyone had, the problem would have been prevented!).

For example, in the downtime argument between production and maintenance presented earlier in this chapter, grasping the current situation would require determining at a minimum:

- The number of downtime hours and incidents that occurred in recent months,
- Which machines accounted for what proportion of the problem (for example, five machines accounted for 81 percent of the department downtime), and
- What, specifically, caused each machine to fail.

In that vein, then, the problem-solver must clarify the problem. The most common first step at Toyota is to travel physically to the actual location (the *genba* ³) where the problem occurred, and observe the situation firsthand. It also means talking with the people involved to find out exactly where the problem occurred, when, and under what conditions. Clarifying the problem further involves finding out why the problem is a problem; that is, what should be happening that is not, or what is not happening but should be? One of the authors was translating for a former general manager of quality at Toyota when an overseas management trainee asked why he should go look at large quality problems on the floor when he would eventually receive a report on the problem later in the week. The act of going and seeing the problem sounded like waste to him. The general manager, Mr. Tomura, answered pointedly by comparing the incidence of quality problems to a murder scene. Unless the investigator looks and sees right away with expert eyes before the scene is contaminated, he or she will not see the evidence that will be needed to catch the criminal. If you want to succeed at Toyota, he sternly lectured, you will treat quality problems like the police do a murder case.

The importance of this act—observing the problem and its context firsthand—is never understated within Toyota. One of the reasons we feel that Toyota places such emphasis on it is that it is a highly effective way to confront one's own assumptions, misconceptions, and biases regarding a certain situation. The problem-solver may think that a certain task (for example, ordering tests in a lab or spare parts in a factory) is done in a certain way but must confirm it through firsthand observation of actual work process. He or she may soon discover that his or her original conception was only approximately correct, that there are a number of exceptions, that only some of the people do it that way, and so forth. Thus, going to the *genba* to observe and to understand is an effective way to verify and update a person's mental image of how the system works, making it more accurate to reality.

Often, as in the hypothetical production-versus-management case from above, where the problem is discovered (on a machine) is not where the problem originated (where and how request forms for spare parts are filled out). As another example, a specimen may arrive at the hospital lab with incomplete orders. The problem was discovered in the lab by a lab technician, but the problem actually occurred in the department where the specimen was extracted and labeled (for example, outpatient services or operating room). The location of problem origination is known as the point of cause. Once the problem-solver has traced the problem back to the point of cause, he or she then should seek to quantify the extent of the problem. How frequently does the problem occur? What percent of units contain this defect? What is the cost impact of the problem? Once quantified, the problem-solver then has a measure to use in checking the results of the problem-solving effort.

Once the problem-solver feels he or she has a sufficient grasp of the current situation, he or she should draw a picture or diagram to illustrate the current situation, process, or system and the problem(s) observed; or, if the situation is not amenable to pictorial representation, describe it in narrative form. The problem-solver can then share this documentation with others involved in or affected by the problem to confirm the accuracy of the picture and/or to add or modify to incorporate new information.

Identifying the Root Cause

At the point of cause, it is usually fairly straightforward to identify the direct cause of the problem. What is the immediate thing that is happening (or not happening) that is creating the problem? This should be confirmed through additional observation or experimentation, as it would be highly unproductive to implement a countermeasure that does not address the problem.

However, the most obvious cause is rarely the root cause. So the problem-solver continues the investigation until a root cause is found, one that if taken care of, would eliminate all future occurrences of the problem. A common method for investigating root cause is the five whys approach. The problem-solver asks, "Why is this problem occurring?" Upon answering it, he or she will have identified a cause to the observed effect. The problem-solver then asks the question again, this time turning the cause into an effect, to identify a deeper cause. The problem-solver continues this inquiry until recurrence can be prevented by addressing that cause. When completed, the problem-solver has a clear and coherent cause-effect chain that demonstrates an in-depth understanding of the problem in context, noting how the root cause is linked to the observed phenomenon. The cause-effect chain should be shared with others to verify that it is probable and reasonable.

In other cases, however, the root cause cannot be deduced from the five-whys technique, and structured tests or experiments are used to eliminate possible causes. For example, one of the authors once investigated a quality problem in the final honing process of a connection rod. The large end crankshaft hole of the connection rod was not staying parallel to the small end hole for connection to the piston pin. He identified six possible explanations for the cause of the problem but could determine the real cause of the problem only by testing each possible cause in careful sequence with measurements at each step of the way. Finally, he confirmed that a previous process was the culprit and the small end hole was not being reamed correctly. A realignment of the spindle head and proper fastening of the bearings in the machine in question solved the problem.

In problems related to organizational processes, we have found Spear and Bowen's articulation of rules for the Toyota Production System (TPS) to be quite useful.[4] From their research, they distilled three rules that seem to govern how Toyota designs its work systems. They are as follows:

- Activities shall be specified according to content, sequence, timing, and outcome.
- Customer-supplier connections shall be clear, direct, and binary.
- Pathways that deliver a product or good shall be simple and direct.

In one of the authors' work on hospital systems, we have not found a single instance where an operational problem did not have, at its root, a violation of one or more of the preceding three rules. In other words, every problem we observed resulted from a poorly specified activity, an unclear connection, or a complicated or undefined pathway. Thus, as a rule of thumb, we would suggest that the root-cause investigation of process-related problems continue at least until one of these rules has been identified.

Devising Countermeasures and Visualizing the Future State

Once the root cause(s) have been identified, the problem-solver can then begin to brainstorm specific changes to the current system that address the root cause(s). Toyota calls these specific changes countermeasures. Often, the countermeasures will be suggested during the course of understanding the current situation and investigating the root cause. The countermeasures should be designed to prevent recurrence of the problem.

This topic of recurrence should not be taken lightly. The overwhelming tendency we find is for people to work around the problem rather than prevent it from recurring. Human nature tends toward the path of least effort. Thus, repair persons will replace a damaged switch or broken valve and view the job as finished, and nurses will find a patient an open bed or call for information that is missing to solve the problem of the now and be done with it. Rarely do organizations put much effort or thought into why the problem occurred in the first place and how to prevent it from ever happening again.

With recurrence prevention countermeasures in mind, the problem-solving team should then give serious consideration to how the new system, process, or procedure will operate with the countermeasures implemented. The future (or target) state should be depicted graphically, illustrating the new system, process, or procedure. Also, at this point, with a deep understanding of the problem and its causes, the problem-solver should be able to predict the extent to which the proposed change will alleviate the problem. This should be made explicit.

Next, the problem-solver should share the envisioned change with key representatives of those groups that will be impacted by it. To the extent possible, the feedback from the affected parties should be incorporated and the revised future (or target) state again shared. Several iterations may be necessary to incorporate as many of the concerns as possible.

Toyota has developed a convention to aid in the feedback gathering and alignment building. Problem-solvers are strongly urged to consider multiple alternative countermeasures for a given problem. Not only does this approach foster creativity in problem solving, but it also gives the other participants more tangible input into the eventual future state. The selection of the final alternative can include the feedback and concerns of all participants, ensuring that the proposed change incorporates a systems viewpoint.

Creating an Implementation Plan

In some organizations, great ideas bubble to the surface only to languish because no clear path to implementation has been laid out. Or great ideas fail to realize their potential because the implementation, rather than the idea, is flawed. So creating an implementation plan is part of a rigorous problem-solving process.

At Toyota, the implementation plan consists of the tasks required to make the envisioned target state a reality (that is, the tasks required to realize and implement the proposed countermeasures), who is responsible for leading that activity, and when that activity will be completed. This is nothing more than an application of the 5W1H principle: stop and check that for each implementation item it is clear exactly Who is going to do What, Where, When, Why, and How. Additionally, the outcome of each task is made explicit (if not obvious) from the description. The problem-solver should create the plan collaboratively so that persons listed in the implementation plan agree to carry out the task by the assigned date.

Creating a Follow-up Plan

A rigorous problem-solving methodology should include a plan for how the actual results will be verified against predicted outcomes. Similar to the implementation plan, the precise activities are made explicit along with the person responsible for making sure each action happens, and dates for when those activities will occur. Although this sounds simple, it is most often not conducted at all.

For example, imagine a change is made to a parts-ordering system or a request for lab tests is altered in response to some problem. After the change, how will we know that the problem is taken care of if we do not quantitatively verify that the countermeasure worked as planned? Did changing the preventive maintenance cycle on the machine result in less downtime? Did the change in the request form result in fewer mistakes? If so, by how much did the problem decrease? If not, then why not?

Follow-up is important for at least three reasons. First, as just indicated, it determines whether the implementation item had any effect. If not, further work and study of the problem remains. Second, the act of follow-up greatly increases the amount of learning that occurs in any given problem-solving event. How do you know that you understood the situation well enough to devise countermeasures that actually work? How do you know that the problem is actually resolved? That is why it is central to the PDCA cycle, and thinking ahead to plan those check activities makes the Check step an intentional action rather than an afterthought. Third, follow-up by key individuals or managers shows that the organization is paying attention to problems and not just letting them slip through the cracks after a discussion meeting.

Discussing with Affected Parties

As figure 2.1 indicates, and as we have noted in the preceding few sections, discussing one's learning and ideas with those affected by the change occurs throughout the Plan phase. Even with those continuous discussions, it is fruitful to approach those individuals again with the whole picture, from diagram of the current situation and diagnosis of root cause through implementation and follow-up plans, to ensure as much alignment as possible. It is possible, for example, that someone originally agreed to a countermeasure but is not agreeable with how the implementation will be carried out. Thus, although the problem-solving effort may be led by an individual, the process must be carried out collaboratively with as broad an audience as is appropriate for the problem.

Obtaining Approval

At Toyota, any change must receive approval before it is allowed. At first glance, such a rule may seem overly bureaucratic, but it actually plays a critical role in the success of the management system once you understand what the approval step represents. First, and perhaps most importantly, the approval step is an explicit mentoring opportunity. Usually the approval must be obtained from one's manager (or manager's manager). This gives the manager the opportunity to mentor the problem-solver, enhance his or her investigative and deductive reasoning skills, help build communication and social networking abilities, and challenge the rigor of the A3 approach. A3 reports actually make mentoring an easier and more accessible task because they make the report author's thought processes visible. Once these thought processes are visible, the mentor can encourage the strong aspects and attempt to shore up the weak aspects.

Second, the approval check ensures the rigor and objectivity of the process, and the depth of understanding attained. Did the investigator visit the *genba?* Does the root cause make sense? Do the countermeasures address root causes? Is the implementation plan realistic? Is the follow-up plan substantive? Did the problem-solver talk with the right people? Are all the right people agreeable to the proposed change? If the problem has not been sufficiently investigated and planned, according to the unwritten rules of the game, the manager will most likely request the problem-solver to do additional work, revise accordingly, and resubmit. On the other hand, even if the manager is doubtful that the countermeasures will affect the problem in exactly the way envisioned, he or she may well approve it anyway as long as the proper process has been followed. The reason is that it represents a learning opportunity, and if all the groundwork has been done to position the person to learn something valuable, why not give him or her the go-ahead?

Executing the Implementation and Follow-up Plans

Upon approval, the implementation plan is executed. To Toyota people, it is critical that the implementation plan be executed according to plan, at least to the extent possible. This is important to separate the effects of the countermeasures and implementation, and to incrementally improve planning skills.

Following implementation, or at times concurrent with implementation, the problem-solving teams execute the follow-up plan to determine whether the change produced the predicted effects. Pending these results, two courses of action are possible. If the results are satisfactory, the new change is established as the standard process and results are disseminated to other groups that may have similar situations (for example, those that use similar equipment).

The perspective here is that the implementation is (to the extent possible) an experiment. If it does not work out, then you return to the old system until you find something better. If the results are not satisfactory, the team engages in an abbreviated problem-solving process to discover why the results were not satisfactory and to take corrective action.

Summary

The problem-solving process illustrated in figure 2.1 and described in some detail in this chapter represents a concrete and tangible approach to implementing the PDCA cycle in an organizational context. The steps outline a very thorough Plan phase, and explicitly call out the Do, Check, and Act phases. At the same time, the problem-solving process demands and elicits the elements of A3 thinking that began this chapter, namely, logical thought processes that demand objectivity, coherence, and synthesis and distillation of information to just the vital points; and a systems approach marked by strong organizational alignment, a consistent problem-solving approach, and an emphasis on process and results to simultaneously improve organizational processes and develop personnel.

With a general process in mind, we now turn our attention to the A3 report. As emphasized earlier, the power of the tool can be realized only when used in concert with the proper thinking and an appropriate problem-solving process to support it. The A3 report is not a documentation format. It is a mechanism to foster deep learning, engaging collaboration, and thoroughness.

Endnotes

1 Also known as the Pareto principle, the 80/20 rule says in essence that most results (more or less 80 percent) spring from a small number (more or less 20 percent) of causes. Similarly, 80 percent of a profit is the result of 20 percent of the products, 80 percent of problems are the result of 20 percent of causes, and so forth.

2 Downtime is the amount of time that a machine is out of service and unavailable for operation.

3 *Genba* (or sometimes *gemba*) is a Japanese word meaning actual or real place. The idea we allude to here has been advocated by other authors, such as M. Imai, Gemba Kaizen (New York: McGraw-Hill, 1997). It is the same concept that Liker describes as *genchi genbutsu* (meaning, "real place, real thing") in *The Toyota Way (2004).*

4 S. Spear and H. K. Bowen, "The DNA of the Toyota Production System," *Harvard Business Review* (September–October 1999): 97–106.

Chapter 3

The Problem-Solving A3 Report

Toyota uses a simple, semistructured one-page document as its primary tool to implement PDCA management across all departments and all levels of the organization. Over many years of practice, Toyota has honed the art of writing these one-page A3 reports to a high level of sophistication. The reports have been transformed from an efficient communication medium to a powerful skill-building and mentorship tool.

The idea of short written reports (such as briefs) as a business or organizational tool is not new. However, short reports seem to have recently fallen out of favor, particularly with the advent of ubiquitous computing, information, and modern presentation technology. We argue that A3 report-style communications (and the commensurate problem-solving and thought processes) are as important now as they have ever been. The amount of information available at one's fingertips is potentially mind-numbing and is growing at geometric rates. This makes the ability to synthesize and distill information to the critically important increasingly vital in today's hypercompetitive environment. Further, the ability to document in a way that speeds communication is equally vital.

A3 reports have been gaining in popularity of late. To our knowledge, this problem-solving tool was first publicized outside of Japan in the course of one of the authors' PhD research.[1] More recent volumes on Toyota have picked up on the tool, providing additional details,[2] and the A3 report has even found its way into the lean health-care movement.[3]

We turn our attention now to the most basic type of A3 report, the problem-solving A3. We describe what actually gets documented on the A3 report during the course of the practical problem-solving process outlined in chapter 2, that is, the content and basic flow of the problem-solving A3. We then include a section on reviewing A3 reports. This section is useful for peers, managers, and mentors as they engage in A3 implementation, with hints on how to review A3 reports to provide substantive mentoring. It is also useful for A3 report authors, as this section can serve as a self-check on one's own report. Finally, we provide you the opportunity to practice what you have learned by describing a case example for which readers are encouraged to draft an A3 report. In subsequent chapters, we address common variations of A3 reports, such as the proposal A3 and the status A3.

Let us take a closer look at the problem-solving A3 report.

Storyline of the Problem-Solving A3

A3 reports are so named because they fit on one side of an A3-sized sheet of paper, roughly equivalent to an 11 x 17-inch sheet. The flow of the report is top-to-bottom on the left side, and then top-to-bottom on the right side, as shown in figure 3.1. A3 reports are thus easily adapted to two A4 (or 8.5 x 11-inch) sheets. Authors write the reports in sections, each clearly labeled and arranged in a logical flow.

According to retired manager Isao Kato of Toyota's Education and Training Department, the A3 summary report tool was heavily influenced by several historical factors. One influence was the emphasis of the basic PDCA cycle for management that was introduced to the company in the 1950s through different channels. Another influence was a formal Total Quality Control (TQC) program launched in 1962 at the insistence of former president and chairman Eiji Toyoda. This program introduced more rigorous methods for statistical quality control and a twelve-step method for summarizing QC circle activities in manufacturing. A third influence was top management's inherent preference for visual control and an inherent dislike of lengthy text-based reports. The now-famous implementation leader of the Toyota Production System, Taiichi Ohno, developed a reputation internally for not reading reports that were longer than a page in length; if he had a question, he insisted upon going to the shop floor to see the problem in person.

These various influences and practices inside Toyota eventually resulted in the creation of a problem-solving and report-writing structure that became a de facto standard called generically the A3, after the size of paper frequently used in the one-page summaries. The earliest A3s were simple problem-solving sum-

Report Theme:

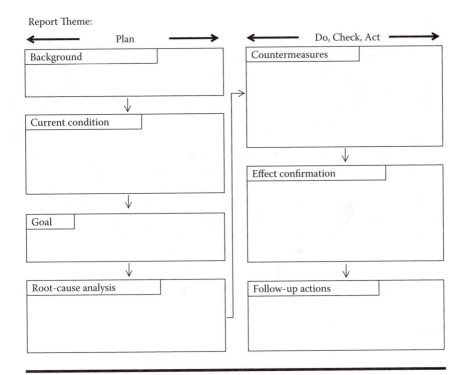

Figure 3.1   Typical flow of the problem-solving A3 report

mary sheets. Later, the tool evolved outwards from this purpose to other applications beyond problem solving and to other departments beyond production.

The A3 report is a flexible tool that can be adapted to fit most problem-solving situations. In order to illustrate the tool's inherent flexibility, we will demonstrate different types throughout this book. However, for a starting point, it is best to understand the flow—what Toyota trainers like to call the storyline—of the original problem-solving A3 report.

The overall flow of the report format embodies the Plan-Do-Check-Act cycle of management. The left-hand side of the A3 is typically devoted to the Plan part of the PDCA by depicting the background of the situation, the current conditions, the goal to be achieved, and the root causes of the problem. The right-hand side reflects the Do, Check, and Act parts of the cycle. The overall balance of the A3 report is no coincidence or accident. The report reflects an often-voiced opinion about problem-solving in Toyota that at least half the effort (if not more) should be put into proper understanding of the situation—that is, the left-hand side of the A3.

The A3 report consists of seven sections, in addition to a theme or title:

- Background
- Current condition and problem statement
- Goal statement
- Root-cause analysis
- Countermeasures
- Check/confirmation of effect
- Follow-up actions

A typical blank report form might look like that shown in figure 3.1. We outline these sections as a teaching template to give the novice A3 author a place to start, but in practice, different sections may be better suited to communicate the author's message. This is okay—in fact, encouraged—as long as the basic storyline (think "PDCA") remains intact. Within Toyota, it is rare to find an A3 report that conforms exactly to the outline we are about to present, yet each follows the basic PDCA storyline and has the same basic elements. It is the thinking, not conformance to a template, that matters. We now explain the process step-by-step, working through an illustrative example as we go.

Theme

Every A3 report begins with a thematic title that introduces the content to the audience. The theme objectively describes the problem addressed in the report and reflects the thematic content of the overall story portrayed to the audience. For example, "Reducing Scrap in the Machine Shop," "Improving Productivity in Stamping," "Improving On-Time Delivery," or "Lead-Time Reduction in Assembly" might be typical titles in manufacturing. In administrative functions or services industries, typical titles might be "Reducing Errors in Accounts Payable" or "Reducing Patient Admissions Time." The theme should help the reader quickly discern the gist of the content. In essence, the theme is the document description. If A3 reports are stored electronically, the theme becomes a searchable text field that would appear in a list of search reports. One can quickly scan the theme statements to zero in on the reports that will have value to a particular question.

A3 report authors may be tempted to see problems through the lens of a particular solution; for example, the problem is that thus-and-such tool is not being used. However, in order to be objective, the theme should focus on the observed problem and not advocate a particular solution. For example, a theme such as, "Hospital Units Calling Instead of E-mailing Inquiries to Pharmacy" predisposes the problem-solving process to a particular solution—getting hospital units to e-mail inquires rather than place phone calls. A better theme would be "Decreasing Turnaround Times by Reducing Pharmacist Interruptions." The broader issue is that pharmacists are being interrupted; reducing the number of phone-call interruptions via an online inquiry system is one possible counter-measure, but there may be others.

Our first example deals with a machine shop that has been incurring significant losses due to poor-quality parts that must be discarded. The scrap rate is well above company goals. The overall aim of the problem-solving effort is to investigate the main sources of defective products and attempt to reduce the scrap rate below the goal set by plant management. For simplicity and communication purposes, we chose the theme "Reducing Scrap Due to Quality Losses in the Machine Shop" and placed it at the top of our A3 report (see figure 3.2)

Background

Having settled upon a title, the A3 report author then should document any pertinent background information that is essential for understanding the extent and importance of the problem. In our experience, two particular items are critical to the background section. First, the author must be acutely aware of

Theme: Reducing Scrap Due to Quality Losses in The Machine Shop

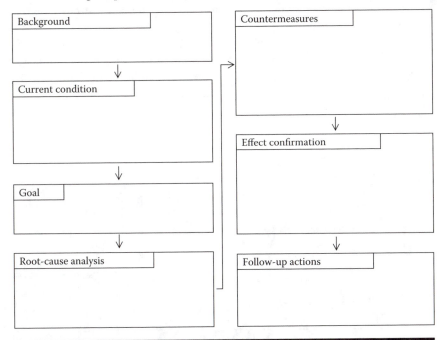

Figure 3.2   Problem-solving A3 template with theme

his or her audience, including their background and informational needs. If the background of the project is not made clear, the audience may not understand what the report is about, resulting in time wasted explaining what the report is trying to accomplish.

Second, tying the background to company goals is also critical. If the A3 report is not related to company's goals in some way, the problem-solver may be wasting time working on a problem that is not very important to the success of the company, and may be considered a poor steward of company resources. Thus, at Toyota, report authors are expected to make an explicit tie to company goals in the background section. Other items that might be included in the background section are how the problem was discovered, the various parties involved, the problem symptoms, past performance or experience, organization structure, and so forth.

Figure 3.3 displays a background section for our "Reducing Scrap Due to Quality Losses in the Machine Shop" A3. It shows that the company-level priorities include improving quality and that this priority flows to the manufacturing-plant level in terms of a fairly aggressive goal for reducing scrap. The writer then foreshadows the problem status by depicting a short historical trend of scrap rates over the past couple of years, indicating that the plant is still well above goals. The report author in this case is trying to make a strong case that this is an important problem for him to be working on, both in terms of his immediate organization's goals for the year and the overall corporate objectives. However, if this report had been written for a different audience, more or less information might be required. For example, if the audience were an executive

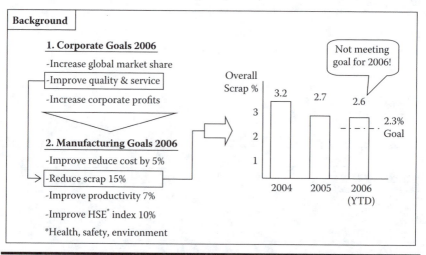

Figure 3.3   Example background section for problem-solving A3 report

from international headquarters rather than local plant management, the author might also include the cost implications of the high scrap rate and the impact on the division's return on investment.

Note also how the author of our case example communicated the background visually rather than purely textually, consistent with A3 thinking. The impact is immediate, and the reader quickly grasps the importance of this report with respect to company goals.

Here are some key points to consider in writing the background section:

■ Make the overall context of the situation as clear and as visual as possible.
■ Identify the target audience and write accordingly.
■ Provide the necessary information that the audience needs to know before going forward.
■ Explain how this topic aligns with company goals.
■ Include any other information, such as historical data, dates, or names that might help the audience understand the importance of this problem.

Written responses to each of these key points are not always necessary, but the astute A3 report author will include the most relevant portions and be ready to explain the gist of the background as needed. As a sample exercise, the report author might consider having only thirty seconds to explain the left-hand side of the report to company executives: How could the background of the situation be summarized in order to avoid wasting their precious time?

Current Condition and Problem Statement

This section is perhaps the most important in the A3 report. The objective is to frame the current condition in a simple way for the reader (not just the writer) to understand. In it, the author draws a visual representation that depicts the critical elements of the system or process that produced the problem. This should involve use of charts, graphs, tables, or other techniques to depict the current condition while avoiding straight text summaries or bulleted lists. A good A3 report paints a clear picture of what is going on and does not simply summarize qualitative opinions. In this section, the author takes time to investigate the facts of the situation and portray them in a visual manner that is helpful to the audience for comprehension.

The chief goal of the current condition section is to provide the audience with a simple (but not simplistic!) overview of the current process and demonstrate a fact-based understanding of the problem. The point of the section is not to tell the audience the "answer" or the author's opinion of what is happening.

Rather, the point is to frame the problem in a useful manner for communication and dialog. One of the key elements of A3 thinking is alignment, gaining agreement on a decision for a specific course of action. Having a picture of the current situation greatly facilitates alignment because the diagram becomes the focus of discussion, with folks literally pointing to the parts with which they agree or disagree, or about which they have questions. The graphical representation serves as a much stronger boundary object to mediate knowledge sharing than does a bulleted list.

In most examples within the current condition section, the problems can be highlighted on the diagram with storm bursts or other demarcations as useful for clarity. Ideally, the material expressed in the current condition should quantify the extent of the problem (for example, percent defects, hours of downtime, and so on) and display this information graphically or numerically. The diagrams should be neatly drawn, readily understandable to any knowledgeable reader, and clearly illustrative of the problem and problem location. When necessary, a specific problem statement can be inserted to frame the problem in words as well. This was a requirement in Toyota A3 training courses for many years.

For our Reducing Scrap problem, the report author collected scrap rate information from all the major departments within the facility. He quantified the overall impact of scrap in terms of cost and found that the largest amount of scrap by far came from the machine shop. He then did additional investigation for the different operations within the machining department to quantify scrap rates and economic impacts. Using this information, he created a visual display that organized the information from best-performing operation to worst-performing department in terms of scrap rate. This information is shown visually and compactly in the current condition diagram displayed in figure 3.4.

The author designed this diagram to make a clear visual connection between his conclusion (grinding is the main culprit of our current scrap-rate situation) and the process used to arrive at that conclusion. Within a few seconds, a reader can quickly discern where the locus of a large part of the scrap rate problem is and at the same time have a good deal of confidence that the investigator was objective in his assessment of the situation.

The data used to develop the current condition diagram should be collected through direct observation in addition to confirmed historical information. Recall from chapter 2 that, in Toyota, an in-depth and detailed understanding of the current process as it is actually performed (not how it should be done or how someone says it is done) is absolutely critical. Workers and supervisors can often describe in theory or in general how the process works or how it is supposed to work, but deviations from this general or hypothetical conception usually hold the key to addressing the problem. For this reason, the data for

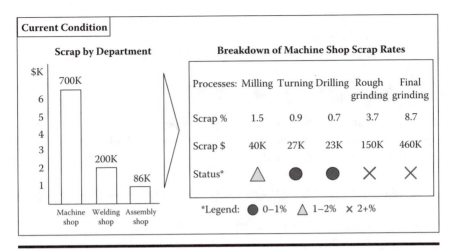

Figure 3.4 Example of current condition section for problem-solving A3 report

describing the extent of the problem should always be actual data, perhaps collected in a logbook, if necessary, and not merely educated guesses.

The benefits of diagramming and quantifying the problem are several. First, the act of drawing a diagram fosters deeper understanding by helping the author compactly organize knowledge and insights gained from observation. Second, the diagram quickly and effectively communicates the core issues to others. It should help present "what is" the problem and, if possible, "what is not" the problem. The graphical medium can contain a very dense amount of information, and yet readers can pick it up quickly because of the pictorial representation. Third, by diagramming the system, problem-solving efforts are focused on the system rather than on the people. This should result in a more objective approach with less defensive posturing.

A final emphasis on the importance of establishing an accurate and objective picture of the current condition is this: Our experience has been that problem-solving efforts fail in implementation most often because the author(s) did not sufficiently understand the current condition. Rarely is failure due to incompetence or lack of ingenuity.

Some key points to consider in drafting the current condition section are as follows:

■ Depict an overview of the current state of the process or system visual.
■ Highlight the key factors in the current state.
■ Identify the real problem in the current state. What is it? What is it not?

- Use quantitative measures to depict the status of the current state (not just qualitative opinions).
- Summarize relevant information pertaining to the current state.

Goal Statement

The goal statement section of the A3 report depends upon the type of problem and type of A3 report. For problem-solving A3s, the goal statement should address at least two fundamental issues:

- How we will know that the project is successful at the end of implementation, and
- What standard or basis for comparison will be used.

Simpler situations may only have one metric to verify success. More complex cases where trade-offs are involved (for example, weight, cost, lead time, and complexity) might involve several metrics.

For the scrap-reduction case we are discussing, it is sufficient to show the current performance of the machines in question and show the target level of performance that the author would like to achieve. The author chose to communicate this information in a simple bar chart, as shown in figure 3.5. In this case, the standard is percent of product scrapped, and we will know whether the project is successful if the scrap rate reduces to 2 percent or better.

In later chapters, we will see that different types of goal statements might make sense as well. In these cases, we might even call it a "target condition" to

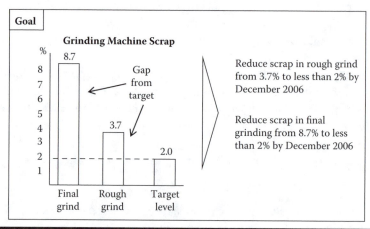

Figure 3.5   Example of goal statement for problem-solving A3 report

be achieved or a "future state" objective instead of a goal. They can both be used effectively once you learn the basic pattern. Regardless, a quantifiable standard against which one can compare results is important to determine whether a change has resulted in improvement.

Here are some key points to consider in drafting the goal statement:

■ Set a clear goal or target state for the situation.
■ Be clear on the measure of performance.
■ Consider how to collect the data to later evaluate and check the effectiveness of any action items.

Root-Cause Analysis

The report author should continue the investigation of the current condition until he or she uncovers the root cause of the problem symptoms identified in the current condition diagram. Failing to address the deeply rooted seed of the problem means it will likely recur. As mentioned in chapter 2, one common technique for root-cause analysis is the 5 Why's method. Using this deductive technique, the problem-solver simply asks a why question approximately five times in series, each time probing the next level of causality. Experience has shown that stopping at two or three whys usually means that the inquiry has not gone deep enough. Finding the root cause may also entail some experimentation. In other cases, an Ishikawa or fishbone diagram might be useful to determine some of the potential root causes.

Toyota's training documentation on A3 reports and problem solving goes to great lengths to emphasize the concept of the 5 Why's method of deduction when it comes to root-cause analysis. From hard work and experience, Toyota practitioners have learned that rarely is the first insight correct and is almost never the ultimate cause of the problem. Thus problem-solvers must develop the discipline of going beyond the superficial level.

To illustrate this point, consider a production downtime problem where a machine stops due to an alarm indication on the control panel. Initial production responses were to reset the overload relay; however, the problem recurred. Eventually, a damaged motor shaft on a pump unit was detected, and the shaft was replaced. Most companies would stop their problem-solving activities here. Unfortunately, in many cases such as this one, that action did not address the root cause of the problem. Odds are high that the problem will reoccur at some point in the future. Only by forcing the discipline of 5 Why's thinking can the problem-solver begin to approach the root cause of the problem.

If we carry the inquiry forward, as illustrated by figure 3.6, several steps are required to get at the real root cause of the problem—that is, metal shav-

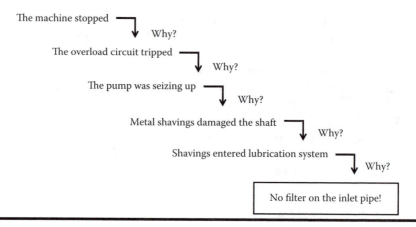

Figure 3.6   Example of the 5 Why's method

ings entering the lubrication system. This deductive-thinking process eventually leads to a better insight that attaching a filter to the lubrication inlet pipe is a suitable countermeasure that should establish true recurrence prevention of the problem. Stopping short of this level would not permanently solve the problem and would only delay its eventual return.

Of course, it is possible to go even further, such as asking why shavings enter the lubrication tank or why shavings are generated in the process at all. However, in this case, the fifth why-level countermeasure of attaching a strainer to the inlet pipe is deemed sufficient to solve the problem. If this were not sufficient, a more thorough countermeasure would be needed. It is the thinking process and ability to determine true cause and effect that is critical. The repetition of asking "why?" over and over helps guide this process.

In practice, real problems often have multiple causes or have causes that are well hidden and cannot be deduced up front using the 5 Why's method. Thus, experimentation may be required to establish cause-and-effect relationships. For this reason, the 5 Why's are not always written out on the A3 report—after all, that would be forcing a process and not requiring thinking. However, root-cause analysis and critical thinking are always probed and challenged during the writing and review process of any A3.

Regardless of the technique used to determine the root cause, the goal of the root-cause analysis section is to show either through logical deduction or experimentation that cause and effect have been established. Most problem-solving efforts fall incredibly short of this goal. Problem-solving teams we have observed often list items that are perceived to be problems without establishing any basic level of proof, or they list items that are easy or popular. This is not acceptable in A3 thinking. Either a cause-and-effect relationship should be established or a structured set of experiments performed to test for cause and effect. Otherwise, the problem-solver is just guessing at the issues and practicing a form of the "ready, fire, aim" school of problem solving.

Figure 3.7 displays an example of a root-cause analysis summarized from the machine shop scrap problem. After further investigation, the report author found that one particular type of problem, undersized shaft arm, accounted for 72 percent of the scrap in the grinding operations. In this case, it turned out that potentially multiple causes contributed to the quality problem. It would be too space-consuming to list several 5 Why's trees, so instead, a fishbone diagram was used to list the main causes potentially contributing to the problem in some fashion. In this case, direct causality has not been determined so countermeasures will be attempted in response to the different perceived causes. Effectiveness will then also be confirmed.

Here are some items to consider in drafting the root-cause analysis section:

■ Be sure to show the root cause of the problem(s) identified in the current state.
■ Separate symptoms and opinions from cause and effect determination.
■ Consider what techniques are most useful for explaining root-cause insight: 5 Why's? Fishbone analysis? Other?
■ Identify what tests might need to be performed in order to establish some level of certainty pertaining to cause and effect.
■ Summarize the main findings of the root-cause analysis, visually, if possible.

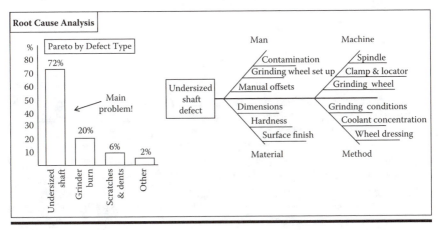

Figure 3.7   Example of root-cause analysis section for problem-solving A3 report

Countermeasures

After root-cause analysis, the problem-solver should have a keen understanding of how the work currently gets done and a good grasp of the root cause(s) of the problems experienced with the system. He or she is now ready to consider how the system might be improved. Toyota calls the improvements "countermeasures" (rather than the ubiquitous "solutions") because it implies both that we are countering a specific problem and that it is what we will use now until we discover an even better countermeasure. The countermeasures address the root cause(s) while conforming to lean design principles.[4] The goal is to move the organization closer to an ideal state of providing exactly what the customer needs, safely, when needed, in precisely the right quantity, and without waste.[5]

The countermeasures section of the problem-solving A3 is a lot like an action list for how the problem or investigation was tackled. Countermeasures are described in terms of "what" (what is the cause of the problem), "how" (how it was investigated or implemented), "who" (who was responsible for this countermeasure), "when" (when was it implemented), and "where" (where was it conducted). "Why" the countermeasure is being conducted should also be clear, if only from context, as well as a plan for how to check and see if the intended effect is achieved or not. For our Reducing Scrap sample A3, the countermeasures section contains a table listing the potential causes, the action taken to investigate each and who was responsible, the date it was done, and the result (see figure 3.8).

Countermeasures

Suspected Cause	Action Item	Responsible	Due	Finding
1. Dirt and contamination	Daily 5S & PM tasks	Tony (T/L)	11/2	Conducting daily. No issues.
2. Grinding wheel set up check	Grinding wheel set up check	Tony (T/L)	11/4	Checked out okay.
3. Manual offset function	Check offset function	Tony (T/L)	11/4	Checked out okay.
4. Spindle bearing loose	Spindle bearing check	Ed (Maint)	11/5	Loose bearing cap. Tightened.
5. Clamp & locator damage	Clamp & locator check	Ed (Maint)	11/5	Nothing abnormal.
6. Grinding wheel balance	Grinding wheel check	Tony (T/L)	11/5	Nothing abnormal.
7. Incoming part dimensions	Measure part dimensions	Janet (QC)	11/9	Within spec.
8. Poor material hardness	Measure hardness	Janet (QC)	11/9	Within spec.
9. Abnormal surface finish check	Surface finish check	Janet (QC)	11/9	Within spec.
10. Grinding conditions abnormal	Grinding conditions check	Mary (Eng)	11/13	Nothing abnormal.
11. Coolant concentration	Measure concentration	John (Maint)	11/13	Contaminated tanks. Replaced.
12. Wheel dressing check	Check conditions	Mary (Eng)	11/13	Nothing abnormal.

Figure 3.8 Example of countermeasures section for problem-solving A3 report

Problem-solvers in Toyota often start the A3 report in the early stages of problem-solving (not just at the end) so they can document, share, and build alignment at each stage. As such, an early version of the countermeasures section can serve as an action plan that outlines who will do what by when. As the various individuals involved carry out the action items, the author updates the section with results. Thus the author may have many versions of the A3, drafted at various stages of problem solving. Typically, only the final "completed" A3, however, is archived.

In an ideal problem-solving world, the root cause would be determined factually in the root-cause analysis section. But in cases where there are several potential or competing causes to the actual problem, the countermeasure section may contain items that are attempted, but that, in the end, wind up not affecting the observed problem. For the sake of completeness, we left all items in the countermeasure plan shown in figure 3.8, as is often done for the sake of learning in A3s. Sometimes it is as important to know what did not work as it is to know what did work.

In other cases, where a physical, procedural, or organizational transformation is involved (such as a new layout, a different flow of information, or a design modification), the author usually draws a diagram of the target condition—that is, a diagram of how the envisioned system will work or the level of desired performance with the countermeasures in place. The countermeasures can be noted on the diagram or listed separately in a table. Like the current condition, any target condition diagram should be neat and clear to all who read the report. An example of this style will be provided as an example of a proposal style A3 (see chapter 4).

Some key points to consider in drafting the countermeasures section are as follows:

- Make sure to address the potential root cause(s) with the action items.
- Identify who will implement the countermeasure.
- Make it clear exactly what will be done.
- Clarify the due date by which action items will be completed.
- Make the implementation order and location clear.

Check/Confirmation of Effect

Nearly every problem-solving A3 contains a section labeled check or confirmation of effect. The reason for this is quite simple. First, A3 reports have part of their intellectual roots in quality control circles that in turn embody the Plan-Do-Check-Act cycle of management espoused by quality leaders such as Walter

Shewhart and W. Edwards Deming. Toyota simply set out to practice what thinkers like these gentlemen strove to teach American management decades ago.

The second reason for the Check phase is to counter the natural tendency of many to skip this crucial step in problem solving. Often, action items are implemented and people just move on. Whether or not the problem has been eliminated or reduced is not verified rigorously. Filling out an effect confirmation section makes the author demonstrate whether the countermeasures have had an effect or not, thus testing his or her understanding of the causes and effects related to the problem being studied.

Two important elements of A3 thinking should be evident in the check section of the report. The first is that the author has used the standard or basis for comparison stated in the goal section. In other words, do we know whether the action items have had an effect or not? Second, and equally important, the check section should establish the causal linkage between the action items and the observed effect. Often teams implement a whole range of action items in response to a problem, and the issue sometimes does go away. However, no one knows exactly why the problem went away or which action item was the most responsible for the problem elimination. Thus, true cause and effect has not been determined. This distinction is critical in A3 thinking: The author should seek to understand cause-and-effect relationships, not just implement a variety of things that help make the problem go away. This usually means actions must be taken one at a time and measurements taken in order to verify which action precipitated the desired effect.

In our ongoing example, the team was able to deduce through experimentation that, of their twelve well-thought-out action items, just two produced the majority of the reduction in the problem: the tightening of the bearing caps and the replacement of the fluid in the coolant tanks. The report author shows this deduction using a time series chart that depicts the decrease in scrap rate and the commensurate timing of the two most effective countermeasures (see figure 3.9).

Here are some key points to consider in drafting the confirmation of effect section:

■ Verify the effectiveness of the action items in total.
■ Use the same standard as the one listed in the goal section.
■ Determine ways to verify the effectiveness of the items, one by one if possible.
■ Plan in advance for the data that will need to be collected.
■ Identify who will help collect the data and how frequently.

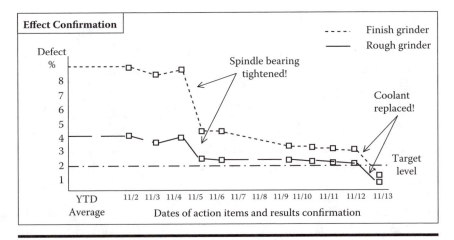

Figure 3.9 Example of confirmation of effect section for problem-solving A3 report

Follow-up Actions

The final section of a problem-solving A3 should reflect the Act step of the PDCA management cycle. The effectiveness of the countermeasures implementation is confirmed in the previous section of the report. In light of learning gained, the intent of the follow-up actions section is to reflect what further changes should be made to the system to sustain the improvement and what remains to be done (that is, issues that have not been investigated but that, in the opinion of the author, should be).

One angle to consider is what must be done to ensure that the gains from the countermeasures are sustained. In the Reducing Scrap example, the two items with the biggest effect were tightening the bearings on the machine, which had become loose with use over time, and contamination of the coolant. Ideally, the bearings should never become loose but perhaps this would require an expensive redesign of the machine. If this is the case, then, at a minimum, a proper preventive maintenance (PM) check interval should be established for these machines. By tightening the bearings and checking the coolant concentricity as part of the machine's routine maintenance, as shown in figure 3.10, the organization can prevent the problem from ever recurring, at least from these two sources.

A second angle to consider in the follow-up actions section is who else should know about this finding in order to expand the improvement. For example, are these similar types of machines used elsewhere in the facility? Are they used anywhere else in the company? Will the company purchase this type of machine again and, if so, how can the design be improved with respect to the problems?

Follow Up Actions			
Investigation Item	**Responsibility**	**Due**	**Status**
1. Establish coolant check PM	Ops & maintenance	11/15	Complete
2. Establish bearing check PM	Ops & maintenance	11/15	Complete
3. Communicate findings to similar plants	Tom eng mgr.	11/22	In-process
4. Discuss bearing issue with OEM	Tom eng mgr.	11/29	Pending

Figure 3.10   Example of follow-up actions section for problem-solving A3 report

If any of these applies, then how can we best communicate these findings to the related parties? In Japanese, Toyota calls this process *yoko-narabi-tenkai*, which is roughly translated, "lateral deployment of findings to related groups." It is an important but frequently overlooked part of the A3 thinking/PDCA process. The key point is to get the information into the hands of other parties who need to know this finding as well. Otherwise, the results merely stay local and are not fully optimized. This is where the compactness and readability of the A3 tool really have an impact, quickly and effectively disseminating new learning to appropriate parties throughout the organization.

Here are some key items to consider in drafting the follow-up actions section:

■ Look for similar processes in the department that can benefit from these countermeasures.
■ Ask whether there are any similar processes outside of the department or plant that should know this information.
■ Consider whether there are any planning departments that should be made aware of the change for the purpose of improving future processes.

Total Effect

Overall, the flow of the problem-solving A3 report follows the practical problem-solving approach described in chapter 2. Starting with the report theme, the author provides pertinent background information for the audience and then depicts the current situation as factually and visually as possible, followed by a root-cause analysis. Next, the author presents the countermeasures used to address the problem and provides data on the results of implementation. The report concludes with reflections on what additional steps should be taken with the learning gained from the problem-solving activities. Figure 3.11 depicts the completed A3 report for the "Reducing Scrap Due to Quality Losses in the Machine Shop" example, with minor formatting modifications.

Reviewing Problem-solving A3s

As the A3 is being drafted, the author collects feedback on his or her analysis of the problem, starting with confirming the background and current conditions, all the way through countermeasures and follow-up actions. He or she integrates as much of the feedback as possible into the report. This is such a strong ethic at Toyota that problem-solvers are expected, as a courtesy, to return to reviewers if unable to incorporate their feedback, and explain why. The cross-functional input is important not just to increase the quality of the report but for considering as many angles as possible (thus strengthening objectivity) and building alignment.

In a company like Toyota that has large numbers of managers who have been trained in this style of thinking and report writing, finding people capable of critical review is quite easy. For many companies, however, this may not be the case. Thus, we have developed a checklist of the most common types of questions asked during an A3 review (see table 3.1). The questions, listed by report section, are typical of those frequently asked either by colleagues or supervisors experienced in reviewing draft A3s. Report authors can use these same questions in self-critique and in anticipation of a meeting. Preparing for a meeting or report session in this way can significantly raise the efficiency of the discussion process. All of the questions may not apply to every A3, and all of this information may not fit on one A3 report. However, Toyota report authors are expected to be prepared to answer these questions verbally if and when they arise.

At Toyota, every A3 report is written and submitted to someone, often a manager or supervisor, who critically evaluates the report, the problem-solving process used, and the results. Most often, the review follows a Socratic-style questioning, using questions similar to those listed in table 3.1, and need not wait until the report is complete. If the manager reviewing a completed report is satisfied, the report is approved, the follow-up actions are carried out, and the A3 report itself is filed for future reference. If the manager is not satisfied with one or more aspects of the report or problem-solving process, the report author is asked to revise and resubmit. For the Toyota manager to be satisfied with a report, it must not only be technically sound but also the author must be able to confirm alignment of all parties who may be concerned (that is, did you go back and talk to that person whose concerns you were not able to fully address?). The approval, then, is a formal act to indicate that the report is complete and ready for archive, and that the organization has achieved agreement on the particular issue. The hard work has been done in the discussions, analysis, experiments, and other activities that are summarized in the report.

At first blush, this may seem like an overly bureaucratic procedure, but the benefits to Toyota are significant. First, it turns the A3 report from a piece of

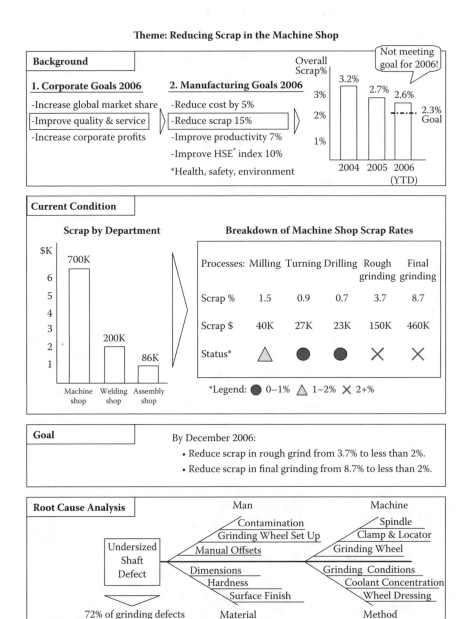

Figure 3.11a   Reducing Scrap example of problem-solving A3 report

To: Chuck O.
From: Art S.
Date: 12/10/06

Countermeasures

Suspected Cause	Action Item	Responsible	Due	Finding
1. Dirt and contamination	Daily 5S & PM tasks	Tony (T/L)	11/2	Conducting daily. No issues.
2. Grinding wheel set up check	Grinding wheel set up check	Tony (T/L)	11/4	Checked out okay.
3. Manual offset function	Check offset function	Tony (T/L)	11/4	Checked out okay.
4. Spindle bearing loose	Spindle bearing check	Ed (Maint)	11/5	Loose bearing cap. Tightened.
5. Clamp & locator damage	Clamp & locator check	Ed (Maint)	11/5	Nothing abnormal.
6. Grinding wheel balance	Grinding wheel check	Tony (T/L)	11/5	Nothing abnormal.
7. Incoming part dimensions	Measure part dimensions	Janet (QC)	11/9	Within spec.
8. Poor material hardness	Measure hardness	Janet (QC)	11/9	Within spec.
9. Abnormal surface finish check	Surface finish check	Janet (QC)	11/9	Within spec.
10. Grinding conditions abnormal	Grinding conditions check	Mary (Eng)	11/13	Nothing abnormal.
11. Coolant concentration	Measure concentration	John (Maint)	11/13	Contaminated tanks. Replaced.
12. Wheel dressing check	Check conditions	Mary (Eng)	11/13	Nothing abnormal.

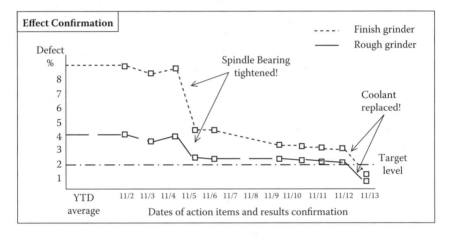

Effect Confirmation

Follow-up Actions

Investigation Item	Responsibility	Due	Status
1. Establish coolant check PM	Ops & maintenance	11/15	Complete
2. Establish bearing check PM	Ops & maintenance	11/15	Complete
3. Communicate findings to similar plants	Tom eng mgr.	11/22	In-process
4. Discuss bearing issue with OEM	Tom eng mgr.	11/29	Pending

Figure 3.11b

Table 3.1 Review Questions for Problem-Solving A3 Reports

Background

Is there a clear theme for the report that reflects the contents?

Is the topic relevant to the organization's objectives?

Is there any other reason for working on this topic (e.g., learning purposes)?

Current condition and problem statement

Is the current condition clear and logically depicted in a visual manner?

How could the current condition be made more clear for the audience?

Is the current condition depiction framing a problem or situation to be resolved?

What is the actual problem in the current condition?

Are the facts of the situation clear, or are there just observations and opinions?

Is the problem quantified in some manner or is it too qualitative?

Goal statement

Is there a clear goal or target?

What, specifically, is to be accomplished?

How will this goal be measured or evaluated?

What will improve, by how much, and when?

Root-cause analysis

Is the analysis comprehensive at a broad level?

Is the analysis detailed enough and did it probe deeply enough on the right issues?

Is there evidence of proper five-whys thinking about the true cause?

Has cause and effect been demonstrated or linked in some manner?

Are all the relevant factors considered (human, machine, material, method, environment, measurement, and so on)?

Countermeasures

Are there clear countermeasure steps identified?

Do the countermeasures link to the root cause of the problem?

Are the countermeasures focused on the right areas?

Who is responsible for doing what, by when (is 5W1H clear)?

Will these action items prevent recurrence of the problem?

Is the implementation order clear and reasonable?

How will the effects of the countermeasures be verified?

Table 3.1 Review Questions for Problem-Solving A3 Reports (*continued*)

Confirmation of effect
How will you measure the effectiveness of the countermeasures?
Does the check item align with the previous goal statement?
Has actual performance moved in line with the goal statement?
If performance has not improved, then why? What was missed?
Follow-up actions
What is necessary to prevent recurrence of the problem?
What remains to be accomplished?
What other parts of the organization need to be informed of this result?
How will this be standardized and communicated?

documentation into a mentoring tool, because the writing of the report makes the report author's thought processes visible. The supervisor can then seize the opportunity to turn from "boss" to "coach" by encouraging the report author in areas where he or she has strengths and by making concrete recommendations in areas that could use improvement. Second, it provides a strong mechanism to ensure that rigorous problem-solving methods are being used and deployed throughout the organization. Third, the A3 review process ensures that members' efforts are targeted in areas that are important for the organization's success, and that actions taken actually do have an impact. Finally, the review step gives managers the opportunity to promote deep learning within their organization and create clear accountability for achieving organizational goals.

Based on our observations of Toyota's system, we feel that an individual can gain a good deal of personal benefit from the exercise of A3 thinking and writing A3 reports. However, in an organization-wide deployment, the greatest benefits will be achieved when a mentoring network and/or approval convention are implemented for the review of A3 reports. Thus, everyone should learn how to write and review an A3 report for the system to achieve full effectiveness.

Your Turn

Now it is your turn. On the next couple of pages we describe a problem-solving situation involving some administrative procedures of a hospital. We are going to violate one of our go-and-see principles here for the sake of learning. In real-world applications, always, always go and observe firsthand to gain a contextualized understanding of the problem. However, we feel that a little practice getting your hands dirty writing an A3 report may be beneficial before tackling a real problem in your organization.

Part 1: Write an A3

The first step of the two-part exercise is to draft an A3 report based on the information provided. In appendix A, we provide a possible "solution" for your reference, along with some explanation of our rationale. We strongly encourage you to not look at our A3 until you have written your own! You cannot learn A3 report writing vicariously. Once you have written yours, you may learn a good deal by comparing what you drafted against the provided countermeasure. Remember, though, there is no one correct A3 report. Our sample is one of many good A3 reports that could be written to accomplish similar purposes.

So, for part 1 of the learn-by-doing exercise, get out an 11 x 17-inch sheet of paper and a pencil (and maybe a big eraser!), and draft an A3 based on the following information. You may find that you would like to have more information than what is provided. If that is the case, make some assumptions and proceed accordingly. Remember, this is for practice in the art of A3 report writing.

> The management of the hospital where this study takes place (let us call it Community Medical) desires to reduce one of its key metrics: accounts receivable (A/R) days, which is the time between rendering a given service and receiving payment for that service. One area of the hospital with higher-than-average A/R days is the Emergency Department (ED). It was discovered that ED charts frequently wait for transcriptions, resulting in delayed bill drops. Bill drop is the time from providing the service until the patient's bill is ready for invoicing.
>
> To actually generate a bill, the patient's medical file (or chart) must be coded, that is, assigned a numerical code for each service rendered for the purposes of insurance billing. Coders need a transcription of the physician's dictation of the visit to ensure the accuracy of the coding and to comply with accreditation regulations. Emergency Department dictations are transcribed by a third party (Ultramed), and the transcriptions are then downloaded in the hospital's Information Management (HIM) Department which does the coding for all hospital patient accounts.

STOP: Before going further, draft a theme statement and background section assuming the audience is the director of financial services (one level below vice president and the HIM manager's boss).

After physically following the route of medical charts through the process and interviewing each person who touches the chart between the ED and billing departments, the team arrived at the following description of how the current process works.

1. Upon discharge, the physician who saw the patient records the dictation over the phone to Ultramed (similar to leaving a voicemail), and then jots an Ultramed job number on the patient's chart.
2. The patient's chart is sent to HIM where it is placed in a file holder.
3. Meanwhile, Ultramed transcribes the dictation and posts it to a limited access Web site.
4. An HIM staff member, who is assigned to periodically check the Web site, prints the transcriptions and places them in a designated location ordered by date.
5. Another HIM staff member periodically matches the stack of transcriptions to the patient charts. If he or she discovers a chart without a job number (meaning a dictation had not been made), the chart goes back to the ED for dictation. A chart with a job number but no transcription requires follow-up with the transcription company.
6. A pool of coders retrieves the completed charts for coding. Occasionally an HIM coder must manage a crisis because the chart is complete for coding, but somehow, the transcription cannot be found. When finished, the coders return the files to the designated location in the file holder for coded charts.
7. The coded charts move to the billing department.

STOP: Now draw a diagram that depicts your understanding of the coding process described above. To test your diagram, show it to someone else to see whether they get it.

One of the problems frequently encountered was that transcriptions could become available from Ultramed, and even downloaded, but would not get matched with patient files. In one day's exception report for delayed bills, seventeen charts were identified as awaiting transcriptions in HIM, but of those, seven transcriptions were already present in the HIM! In other words, seven transcriptions had been made but had somehow become lost or misplaced in the system, thus delaying bill processing on those accounts. Thus, patient files waited in queue unnecessarily, resulting in delays in authorization to send bills and increasing A/R days. In addition, HIM staff spent significant effort keeping track of patient files and transcriptions, following up on late dictations and so forth.

The bill drop time for this process ranged from seven days to over fifty days, with an average of ten days. Based upon conversations with multiple parties, including the fiscal services management team, it was decided that a target bill drop rate of seven days or less would be reasonable.

STOP: What would be a good goal statement for this problem? Write it. Also add the measurement data on delayed charts pictorially to the current condition diagram.

As the team investigated why chart coding was being delayed, it became clear that the complexity of pathways made it difficult for the HIM staff to manage the flow of charts through its department. No one could see easily where charts needed go next. The complexity meant that the person responsible for matching transcripts to patient charts often failed to do so. The most common reason for this was that the person did not see or find the transcript. Transcriptions were missing or not found for many reasons: they were out of order; physicians delayed getting dictations made; the staff failed to realize that outstanding transcriptions had to be made; and a mixing up of recent and outstanding transcriptions had occurred, among others. After sifting through the various causes, it became apparent that the main cause of this confusion was that the system lacked clear signals for indicating when ED physicians had done their dictations and when transcriptions were ready for download.

STOP: Draft a root-cause analysis section for the A3.

After considering a number of options, the team decided to improve the sequence of the work flow. The primary countermeasure selected was to receive the transcriptions in the Emergency Department and mate them with patient charts before sending them to HIM. This would eliminate the set of work-around loops in HIM altogether and cut down confusion because the Emergency Department is in a much better position to manage the relationship with Ultramed (they know more readily whether a dictation has been made and when). The overall process becomes greatly simplified even though some of the work shifted from the HIM department to the ED. Moving receipt of transcriptions to the ED meant a change to the ED work processes, but it represented little added workload.

STOP: Draw a diagram depicting how this new process would work. Be sure to label the countermeasures clearly. Also, note that the countermeasures involve changes in the ED, not just in HIM, and to physicians' routines. Thus, an important member of the audience is the chief medical officer who oversees all ED physicians as well as ED operations. So, return to the previous sections to see whether any revisions are needed now that the chief medical officer will be among the intended audience.

An implementation plan was then devised for minimal disruption and maximum likelihood of success. A critical step was to work with the Information Systems Department to set up the necessary hardware and network link within the ED. M. Ghosh was put in charge of this step with a due date of August 7, 2005. The remaining steps were to communicate the change to the ED doctors and train ED and HIM staff in the new procedures. S. Moore took responsibility to interface with ED physicians by August 12 and train ED staff by August 15, 2005. K. Wells agreed to train the HIM staff by August 26.

The problem-solving team had hoped that 100 percent of charts would reach HIM with transcriptions, and that time from seeing patient to authorization to send out the bill (bill drop time) would become seven days or less. Six weeks after implementation, data were gathered on two weeks' worth of patients. Out of 371 charts over a two-week period, over 98 percent arrived with transcriptions, and bill drop time averaged 6.55 days.

STOP: Draft a section reporting the action plan and results. What would be the most suitable heading for this section?

The team also came up with three main follow-up actions to work on in the future. One was to determine the cause of the few charts still arriving into HIM without a transcription and to search for a remedy. Another was to seek out ways to further reduce the bill drop rate and to reduce the amount of time required to code the charts. Last, the team agreed it was necessary to continue to verify with the Billing Department that the coding continued to be accurate.

STOP: You are nearly done! Write up a follow-up actions section.

Now, to complete the A3, compile all the sections onto one 11 x 17-inch sheet of paper. You can now compare it to the sample A3 in appendix A for some improvement ideas.

Part 2: Critique Your A3

Now that you have written your A3 (and possibly taken a peek at the A3 we wrote for this case study), we suggest a bit of self-critique. Based upon the information we provided on reviewing A3s, use the prompting questions to critically evaluate your A3 report. If you prefer, critique ours! We have provided our own critique in appendix A. Again, it is probably most beneficial to your learning for you to do your own critique before looking at the "answers." Again, there is no right or wrong answer. So if you arrive at a different conclusion than we did, that is okay! The important thing is to begin exercising A3 thinking.

Summary

In this chapter, we introduced A3 report-writing and summary techniques in greater detail by the use of examples. There is no one way to write an A3, and no two ever look quite the same. In the next two chapters, we explain even more variety beyond just the basic problem-solving A3. However, keep in mind that although there will be variety in the creation of A3s, they do adhere to some very important common tenants.

- Perhaps most obviously, A3 report authors strive to display the contents on a single A3-sized sheet of paper and not on dozens of pages or PowerPoint slides.
- A3 report authors attempt to depict the condition and analysis of the problem in a visual manner, not just with text.

■ The report structure always follows some derivative of the Plan-Do-Check-Act style of management, probably the most critical of all points we have discussed.

Finally, remember that A3s are simply a tool for communication and guiding improvement. They are not an end state in and of themselves and merely part of the improvement process. Do not fall into the trap of assuming that every problem or project needs to be summarized in this fashion—you will run out of time and never complete anything.

Endnotes

1 D. K. Sobek II, J. K. Liker, & A. C. Ward, "Another Look at Toyota's Integrated Product Development," *Harvard Business Review* (July–August 1998): 36–49.

2 See, for example, J. K. Liker, *The Toyota Way* (New York: McGraw-Hill, 2004); and J. Morgan and J. K. Liker, *The Toyota Product Development System* (New York: Productivity Press, 2006).

3 See D. Weber, C. Jimmerson, and D. K. Sobek, "Reducing Waste and Errors: Piloting Lean Principles at Intermountain Healthcare," *Joint Commission Journal on Quality and Patient Safety* (May 2005): 249–57.

4 Lean process design principles can be found in any of the numerous books and articles on lean manufacturing or the Toyota Production System, such as Y. Monden (1998), *Toyota Production System, An Integrated Approach to Just-In-Time* (Norcross, GA: Engineering & Management Press, 1998). A particular favorite of one of the authors, as mentioned in chapter 1, is Spear and Bowen's Four Rules in Use.

5 This description of Toyota's notion of "ideal" was first articulated by Spear and Bowen, "Decoding the DNA of the Toyota Production System," *Harvard Business Review* (September–October 1999): 97–106.

Chapter 4

The Proposal A3 Report

In the preceding chapter, we introduced the basic A3 tool used for problem solving. In teaching A3 report writing, Toyota starts with that version and ensures that employees use it in appropriate situations throughout their early career development. One of the authors went through repeated learning cycles of this process for several years while working for Toyota in Japan. Obviously, an A3 report cannot be written for every problem or situation in life. But Toyota uses it frequently where clarifying problems experienced during the course of work and where resolving the problem leads to useful and important learning opportunities. We suggest that adopters of this method also practice the problem-solving A3 report first, as it is the most generally applicable form of the tool.

That said, however, there is no single right way to write or even frame an A3 report. Each is unique in content, and even the framing mechanism changes in many cases. Why? In real life, organizations face a variety of situations beyond just standard problem solving. In this chapter, we introduce another way to frame an A3 report: for the purpose of making a proposal.

Good proposal writing requires excellent problem-solving skills, so at first blush, it may seem that we do not need separate formats. However, proposals have several key differences that are substantial enough to warrant separate discussion. Problem-solving A3s are typically written after the Plan, Do, and Check steps of the PDCA cycle (although authors often start them earlier in the problem-solving process). The report captures the root cause(s) of the observed problems, confirms that the problem was resolved, and reflects on the problem-solving efforts. The report author typically needs approval before proceeding to the Act step, which involves archiving the report, disseminating the findings and recommendations, and/or changing procedures.

Proposal A3s, on the other hand, are written during the Plan step and before the Do step. The reason is that proposal A3 reports address situations where the investment is significant (either in financial or human capital), the implementation is fairly involved, and/or the recommendation is far-reaching across the organization. As such, proposal A3 reports typically address issues such as policy, management practice, organizational processes, or any situation where the organization would like careful consideration, planning, and (to the extent possible) consensus on the recommendation before making a decision or authorizing action. Technically, proposals may not address a problem per se but rather an opportunity or a need to change or improve. A decision on whether to outsource certain components, a policy on employee training, or a decision to change health-care benefits might all be considered a policy.

Regardless of the differences, however, each type of A3 report still follows the basic PDCA cycle. The planning starts by clearly defining the current situation and reasons for change. The actual proposal includes analysis, frequently involving comparisons of several alternative approaches. The implementation plan includes both confirmation of effect (Check) and follow-up (Act) steps. The expectation is that, upon implementation, the team will collect data to evaluate its effectiveness and reflect and act on any needed revisions before going forward. Often, the Check and Act steps are summarized in a status A3 report, the subject of chapter 5. Table 4.1 summarizes the key differences between problem solving and proposal writing to help clarify the differences.

The differences may be subtle but are important. In particular, the problem-solving reports tend to center more on typical metric-related themes such as quality, cost, delivery, productivity, and lead time. These A3s are practiced early in the career of young employees in Toyota in order to develop the skills of critical thinking and problem solving. Later, as employees progress in management or gain more experience, the nature of work changes. It is less reactive to day-to-day activities and more oriented toward the future and upcoming changes; thus, the employee is better positioned to make sound proposals. Finally, the analysis portions of problem-solving reports are focused on identifying and resolving the root cause(s) of problem observed in daily work and typically involve quantitative or analytical models. Proposals also involve analysis, and Toyota mentors encourage proposal writers to quantify as much of their analyses as possible. But because proposals typically deal with larger-scope issues such as policy or organizational changes, the analyses often also include qualitative assessments.

Regardless of industry sector, managerial and professional work involves altering policies and seizing opportunities for improvement. The next section presents a general outline for proposal A3 reports. We present the proposal A3

Table 4.1 Comparison of Problem-Solving and Proposal A3 Reports

Focus	Problem solving	Proposal writing
Thematic content or focus	Improvements related to quality, cost, delivery, safety, productivity, and so on	Policies, decisions, or projects with significant investment or implementation
Tenure of person conducting the work	Novice and continuing throughout career	Experienced personnel and managers
Analysis	Strong root-cause emphasis; quantitative/analytical	Improvement based on considering current state; mix of quantitative and qualitative
PDCA cycle	Documents full PDCA cycle involved in making an improvement and verifying the result	Heavy focus on the Plan step, with proposed Check and Act steps embedded in the implementation plan

report in template form to help get first-time users started, but we also emphasize that, like snowflakes, no two A3s are exactly alike. Thus, we will follow with two examples that demonstrate the flexibility of the tool and how the basic outline can be adapted to suit particular situations. We encourage first-time A3 report authors to use one of the example outlines as a starting point for your reports and to adapt as needed for the particular situation. We conclude the chapter with a practice exercise as we did in chapter 3.

Let us now take a closer look at the proposal A3 report.

Storyline of the Proposal A3

Proposal A3 reports are the same shape and size as problem-solving A3s. Both fit on one side of an A3-sized (or 11 × 17-inch) sheet of paper. The flow is still top-to-bottom on the left side, then top-to-bottom on the right side, as shown in figure 4.1. And like their problem-solving counterpart, proposal A3s are written in sections, each clearly labeled and arranged in a logical flow.

Report Theme:

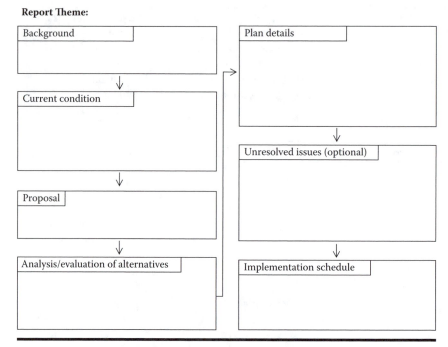

Figure 4.1   Typical flow of the proposal A3 report

Proposal A3s still follow the same basic PDCA structure of problem-solving A3s; however, because it is a proposal, the latter steps of the cycle are still pending at the time of writing. The goal of the proposal A3 is to present a logical, structured plan for consideration so that a good decision on implementation can be made. The plan to implement, check, and follow-up are expressed in writing so there is no ambiguity or confusion as to what is proposed and who will carry out various parts of the plan. In some cases, teams propose a pilot study to try out the proposed ideas or changes on a small scale before full implementation. We will work through a simple example for practice and use it to help explain step-by-step the process and inherent thinking pattern.

Theme

Like the problem-solving A3, the proposal A3 report begins with a thematic title that introduces the content to the audience. The theme should objectively describe the proposal addressed in the report, while clearly indicating that it is a proposal. For example "Food Service Outsourcing Implementation," "Proposal to Change Tooling Vendors," and "Health and Benefits Plan Recommendation" might be typical titles. Regardless of the industry or situation, the theme should convey to the reader at a quick glance what the content is all about.

Our proposal example comes from an organization that employs approximately 200 professionals. The technical departments must frequently purchase materials and supplies using a typical purchase order process.[1] The purchasing and finance departments would like to recommend the use of corporate credit cards to purchase low-dollar-amount items in order to streamline the process. Thus the theme chosen for this A3 is "Corporate Credit Card Implementation."

Background

Having settled upon a theme, the A3 report author should convey any pertinent background information that is essential for understanding the extent and importance of the problem or opportunity and how it relates to company goals or values. The more varied the audience that will read the report, the broader the background information will need to be.

Figure 4.2 shows a background section for our Corporate Credit Card Implementation A3. In this case, the pertinent background information is summarized in a few bullet points to put the next section (current condition) in context. Particularly, the author highlights that administrative head count is likely to grow along with organization growth unless more efficient systems can be implemented; that the current system is largely paper-based and therefore slow and cumbersome; and that $100 purchase orders (POs) require the same amount of processing expense as $100,000 POs. Although no company goals are explicitly identified, it clearly plays to the company goals of reducing costs and improving productivity of internal operations.

The purpose and content of the background section of the proposal A3 is similar to that of the problem-solving A3. We reiterate the key points here for convenience:

■ Make the overall context of the situation as clear as possible.
■ Identify the target audience and write accordingly.

Background

- Company anticipates growth through the next 5–10 years; administrative overhead will also increase without efficiency gains.
- Current paper-based system for processing purchase orders (POs) does not take advantage of new financial technologies.
- Emergency and spot transactions are currently burdensome and time consuming.
- All purchases are treated the same, regardless of dollar amount.

Figure 4.2   Example of background section of a proposal A3

- Provide the necessary information that the audience needs to know before going forward.
- Explain how this topic aligns with company goals.
- Include any other information, such as historical data, dates, or names, that might help the audience understand the importance of this problem.

Current Condition

Just as with the problem-solving A3, this section is critically important. The objective is to frame the current condition in a simple yet accurate way for the reader (not just the writer) to understand what is going on currently and to motivate the need for the proposal. Ideally, the author draws a visual representation that depicts the key elements of the current condition. This message should involve the use of charts, graphs, tables, or other techniques to depict the current condition.

In the Corporate Credit Card Implementation proposal, the report authors collected data about how much it costs to process purchase orders and invoices for the key departments involved in such transactions. They also gathered data on how many purchase orders were processed in the preceding years for several categories. As shown in figure 4.3, some of the information is displayed graphically to clearly convey the point that a large percentage of POs account for a small percentage of total PO expenditures. Other information is displayed in tables because the data are used in the analysis section of the report. Together, the data as presented communicate the potential to streamline these low-dollar

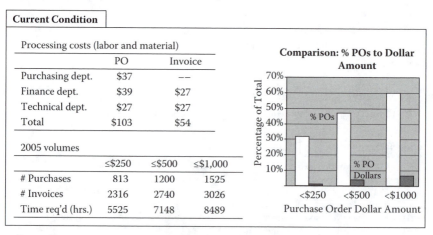

Current Condition

Processing costs (labor and material)

	PO	Invoice
Purchasing dept.	$37	––
Finance dept.	$39	$27
Technical dept.	$27	$27
Total	$103	$54

2005 volumes

	≤$250	≤$500	≤$1,000
# Purchases	813	1200	1525
# Invoices	2316	2740	3026
Time req'd (hrs.)	5525	7148	8489

Figure 4.3 Example of current condition section of a proposal A3

expenditures and the relatively small risk to the company in changing proce-dures.[2] As with earlier A3 examples, the material is organized so that even a casual reader can quickly discern the basic situation.

As before, the key points to consider in drafting the current condition section are similar to the problem-solving A3, but are repeated here for convenience:

- Clearly depict an overview of the current condition in a visual manner.
- Highlight the key factors in the current state.
- Identify the main issues in the current state for the reader.
- Use quantitative measures to depict the status of the current state (not just qualitative opinions).
- Summarize relevant information pertaining to the current condition.

Analysis and Proposal

After the depiction of the current condition, the flow of the proposal A3 can take any of a number of directions depending on the nature of the proposal. One common pattern is to conduct an analysis of the current condition, in a similar vein as the problem-solving A3 reports described in chapter 3. The concepts of data collection, direct observation of the process, and root-cause thinking still apply very much. However, because some proposals deal with future states or conditions that often are not as clear, it is not always possible to conduct or write the analysis section in the same way. Thus the analysis in proposal A3s tends to be less quantitative. However, the analysis should still be systematic, thorough, and quantified to the extent possible. The analysis section then leads to a set of alternative approaches, frequently presented in a matrix that compares the alter-natives along several key dimensions. (We will illustrate an evaluation matrix in a case example later in the chapter.) The proposal section concludes with the author's recommendation.

In another common pattern, the current condition leads directly to a pro-posal statement, and the author presents an analysis of the proposal rather than the current condition. This pattern often occurs when the current state is not experiencing problems per se, but the author has identified an opportunity that could provide significant benefit to the company.

Our Corporate Credit Card Implementation example A3 follows this sec-ond pattern (see figure 4.4), because the authors have identified an improve-ment opportunity by taking advantage of a product offered by a vendor (in this case, corporate purchasing credit cards offered by a national bank). They do not conduct an analysis of alternatives, because the decision is whether to adopt this product company-wide. It is also possible that they were asked by the vice president of administration to look into getting credit cards for the purchasing

Proposal		
Implement use of purchasing credit cards for purchases ≤$500 to incur cost savings and increases in efficiency through: • Reduced labor hours in Tech Groups, purchasing, and finance • Reduced PO, RFP, expense report, invoice paperwork		

Cost and Time Analysis

	PO	Invoice
Labor and material cost savings		
Current cost per transaction	$103	$54
Est. purchasing card costs	$20	$20
Savings per transaction	$83	$34
Potential annual cost savings	$99,600	$93,160
Time savings (hours)		
Current PO system	3,300	3,900
Est. purchasing card	650	1500
Potential annual time savings*	2,650	2,350
* Approx. 1/3 of time savings is to Tech Groups		

Figure 4.4   Example of analysis and proposal sections of a proposal A3 report

department and make a proposal. Following the current condition is a concise proposal statement, followed by a fairly compelling analysis of the time and cost savings of the proposal.[3]

Here are some items to consider in drafting the analysis section of proposals:

- Be sure to show the main cause of the problem(s) in the current state.
- Separate symptoms and opinions from cause and effect determination.
- Highlight what is wrong or what needs to be changed.
- Show why the current process or situation can be improved.
- Build a logical case for change in order to move the proposal forward.

Some key points to consider in drafting the proposal section are:

- Clearly state the proposal that you are making for the audience.
- List the main alternatives that are up for consideration.
- Evaluate the alternatives in some fashion, ideally quantitatively.
- Identify the most suitable path for moving forward.
- Give a clear reason why this option is the best.

Plan Details

No proposal A3 can be complete without a well-thought-out plan regarding the most salient details of the proposal. Here, the author articulates more specifically how the proposed change will function upon implementation. This section commonly incorporates the feedback from multiple parties—ideally from all those affected by the proposed change.

In the corporate credit card example, the plan details section of the report (figure 4.5) is fairly extensive, dealing with policy relating to the issuance and use of purchase cards, a preliminary purchasing procedure using the cards, and

---

Implementation Details

- Dept. manager determines which associates are issued cards for specific dept. purchases.
- Purchasing is issued cards.
- Acceptable business-related purchases using card:

Small tools	Seminars	Photo processing and film
Auto supplies	Office supplies	Postage
Minor equipment repairs	Printer services	Copy services
Electrical supplies	Safety supplies	Building maint. supplies
Catering	Florists	Coffee services
Hardware	Signage	

- Unacceptable uses of card (blocked):

Personal use	Cash advance	Travel & entertainment
Computer hardware	Capital purchases	Indep. contract services
Jewelry, furriers		

- All card users required to sign a purchasing card agreement stating that all use of the card will be for business purposes and within the procedures set forth.

New purchasing procedure:
1. Card user obtains approval from dept. manager for each purchase.
2. Card user contacts vendor, places orders, and provides vendor with appropriate information.
3. Goods shipped as specified and labeled "Purchasing Card"– cardholder name.
4. Goods received per standard receiving procedure with the following exception: packing list and receipt is forwarded to card user.
5. All packing lists and receipts are retained by requestors and matched against monthly statement.
6. Card user reviews statement, attaches appropriate packing lists and receipts, records JRM #'s, signs and forwards to dept. manager.
7. Dept. manager reviews statement for accuracy and initials and dates statement.
8. Dept. manager forwards to finance dept. Finance audits statement and supporting documents for compliance, sales tax, 1099.
9. Finance dept. pays from master invoice received directly from the purchasing card bank.

Controls:
- Monthly dollar limits per card
- $500 single transaction limit
- Limited number of transactions per card per day
- Merchant category blocking (i.e., cash advances, jewelry stores, appliances, etc.)

Figure 4.5   Example of plan details section of a proposal A3 report

various controls to be established that will limit the company's risk. It seems, in the A3 authors' estimation, that the details of how the purchasing card system would work were the most important aspects of the proposal for the audience; therefore, they have chosen to allocate the most space to it.

Unresolved Issues (Optional)

Often, a number of issues related to a proposal may remain unresolved at the time of writing because the content is dealing with the future. For this reason, some authors include an unresolved issues section. For example, sometimes personnel are affected by policy changes, budget issues, or other factors that must be considered. If possible, they should be addressed as part of the proposal presented in the body of the A3, but this is not always possible. Rather than ignoring or dismissing them, a parking lot is created to store potential issues, problems, or points of concern. If appropriate, mitigation of these factors may be included in the implementation schedule. No unresolved issues have been identified in our case example, partly because the proposal details section is so extensive.

Some key points to consider in drafting the unresolved items section are as follows:

- Look for potential roadblocks or areas of concern.
- Consider whether any stakeholders who are affected in some manner have concerns that will need to be addressed.
- Consider unresolved issues relating to budget, training, and shifts in responsibility.

Implementation Schedule

The last main section of the report is a high-level plan on how to move forward. Typically, a proposal A3 does not contain a detailed step-by-step implementation plan but rather a timeline (or timetable) of the main implementation steps planned should the proposal be approved. In most cases, an outline of the key implementation steps is usually sufficient for the audience to assess the difficulty or feasibility of the proposal.

The implementation schedule should answer, in general terms, the following questions:

- What exactly needs to be done?
- Who needs to be involved?
- How will this be attempted at first?
- Where will it be attempted?
- When will it be attempted?

- What preparations must be made?
- How will progress be evaluated?
- When will the reviews for follow-up be held?

An implementation schedule for the Corporate Credit Card Implementation example is shown in figure 4.6.

The goal of this important section is to outline a basic schedule so that implementation will occur in a structured and organized fashion consistent with A3-style thinking. Because this is a proposal to implement change and not a complete report of how the change was implemented, the entire proposal is really a subset of the Plan part of PDCA, with the "Do," "Check," and "Act" steps embedded in the implementation schedule. Often, as with this A3, report authors suggest a pilot as a logical way to test the proposal.

In the case example, the Check and Act phases of the PDCA cycle appear within the implementation plan. Following management approval on September 3, a pilot will be conducted and evaluated (the Check step). The results of evaluation will inform changes to the program before full implementation (the Act step). The implementation schedule includes only the main highlights of the plan; however, it is clear that much thought has gone into the plan as the timeline takes weekends and holidays into account. In chapter 5, we will review A3 reports on project review that capture the Do, Check, and Act steps during or after implementation.

Some key points to consider in drafting the implementation section are as follows:

- Identify the major action items for the proposal to move forward.
- Identify who will be involved and where the implementation will take place.
- Establish the basic timing for the scheduled items.
- Include how progress will be checked.
- Schedule one or more reflection meetings to evaluate progress.
- Determine what standard or basis for comparison makes sense.
- Plan in advance for the data that will need to be collected.

Timeline									
9/3/2006	9/4–9/20	9/16–11/15	11/18–3/31	11/18–3/31	4/1–4/15	4/16–4/18	4/21–5/30	6/2/2007	
Present at cb mtg.	Policy guidelines, issuer selection, supplier enrollment	Training for Pilot: facilities, purch/fin, management	Pilot program	Concurrently revise policy and procedures	Audit, analyze 3 mo. Pilot	Report audit results	Training: company-wide	Company-wide implementation	

Figure 4.6   Example of implementation schedule section of a proposal A3 report

Total Effect

Overall, the flow of the proposal A3 follows the practical problem-solving approach described in chapter 3. Starting with the report theme, the author provides pertinent background information for the audience and depicts the current situation as factually and visually as possible. The proposal presents a clear, concise proposal or recommendation and includes a quantitative or qualitative analysis of either the current state (which leads to the proposed alternatives) or the proposed change (which justifies the proposal). The report author will typically then outline key details that will be essential for others to agree with the idea and an implementation schedule that includes the Do, Check, and Act steps of the PDCA cycle.

Figure 4.7 depicts the completed A3 report for the Corporate Credit Card Implementation example. There are, of course, other ways the report could have been written, since the proposal-writing format has inherently more flexibility than the problem-solving A3s; in fact, many proposal A3s do not follow this exact format or structure. The important thing is that the author has engaged in A3 thinking and has written a proposal that is coherent and organized, and flows well from beginning to end in a way that is consistent with A3 thinking and PDCA. To illustrate the adaptability of the A3 tool, we will now present two proposal A3 report examples with varying organizations and presentations.

Proposal A3 Example 1

Figure 4.8 displays another example of a proposal A3 for further study. This example deals with a company that stopped its food service operations some time ago. To meet growing business needs, a new engineering building was budgeted and approved to be added onto a facility known as "1555," which is simply its street address. The A3 proposal shown was written to consider the options and make a recommendation for reestablishing food service operations commensurate with the expansion of operations. This example deviates from the basic pattern for proposal A3s summarized in the previous section, illustrating that the template shown in figure 4.1 should serve as a rough guide rather than a strictly enforced outline. Let us walk through the example step-by-step at a high level while discussing the differences.

For starters, the background and current condition sections of the A3 were merged into one section. In general, the background section provides the audience with the reasons why this topic is relevant, while the current condition section is more concerned with what the process or situation actually is. In this case, the audience is clearly an internal party familiar with the background and current situation. Detailing the current state is not the key issue—presenting and evaluating available options is—thus, a few bullets to summarize the key background/current condition items is sufficient for this particular audience. In general, though, we recommend erring on the side of more information rather than less on the background/current condition, because most people have a strong tendency to jump to solutions before really understanding the issues.

The next section of the A3 outlines three possible options for reestablishing food services. The author uses an evaluation matrix to concisely convey the major points of consideration and to portray a comparative analysis. At Toyota, consideration of multiple alternatives for almost any decision is so strongly engrained that it is almost mandatory.[4] Evaluation matrices make both the options and the selection criteria visible and help ensure careful and objective consideration of the alternatives against the most important criteria. And because they convey a lot of information concisely, we highly recommend their use. In this example, the matrix compares three options according to nine evaluation criteria and two cost categories. The section concludes with a rough timeline of the decision-making process and overall project timing. The timeline is more suitable here than at the end of the report because it is generic to all three alternatives.

In place of a more typical analysis section, this proposal instead relies upon a benchmarking analysis of six reasonably similar facilities. This type of comparative analysis is typical in cases when the topic is common and external data are available. In this case, the comparison involves similar local companies and affiliated companies. This comparison provides a good sense of what is typical for the type of service provided at other facilities and conveys a strong sense that the author has researched the options carefully.

This example then flows into an unresolved issues section. The author of the proposal identifies three categories of issues related to growth, flexibility, and facilities that have not been resolved by the proposal contents. The unresolved issues are (mostly) common to all three options and reflect issues that the author wants the audience to consider in the decision-making process.

This example concludes with a recommendation section, not an implementation schedule. The reason is because the main purpose of this A3 was to present the options and make a recommendation for consideration (option II and the primary and secondary reasons why option II was recommended). It is very likely that, once a decision is made, much of the body of the A3 would be reused to construct a more thorough implementation plan for the proposal selected, perhaps in the form of a more narrowly focused proposal A3 where the option chosen is taken as the starting point, and the author proposes an implementation plan.

Purchasing Card Implementation

Background

- Company anticipates growth through the next 5–10 years; administrative overhead will also increase without efficiency gains.
- Current paper-based system for processing purchase orders (POs) does not take advantage of new financial technologies.
- Emergency and spot transactions are currently burdensome and time consuming.
- All purchases are treated the same, regardless of dollar amount.

Current Condition

Processing costs (labor and material)

	PO	Invoice
Purchasing dept.	$37	––
Finance dept.	$39	$27
Technical dept.	$27	$27
Total	$103	$54

2005 volumes

	≤$250	≤$500	≤$1,000
# Purchases	813	1200	1525
# Invoices	2316	2740	3026
Time req'd (hrs.)	5525	7148	8489

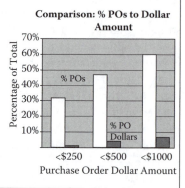

Proposal

Implement use of purchasing credit cards for purchases ≤$500 to incur cost savings and increases in efficiency through:
- Reduced labor hours in Tech Groups, purchasing, and finance
- Reduced PO, RFP, expense report, invoice paperwork

Cost and Time Analysis

	PO	Invoice
Labor and material cost savings		
Current cost per transaction	$103	$54
Est. purchasing card costs	$20	$20
Savings per transaction	$83	$34
Potential annual cost savings	$99,600	$93,160
Time savings (hours)		
Current PO system	3,300	3,900
Est. purchasing card	650	1500
Potential annual time savings*	2,650	2,350

* Approx. 1/3 of time savings is to Tech Groups

Figure 4.7a Corporate Credit Card Implementation example proposal A3 report

To: J. Griffin, VP Admin.
From: Finance & Purchasing
Date: 8/20/2006

Implementation Details

- Dept. manager determines which associates are issued cards for specific dept. purchases.
- Purchasing is issued cards.
- Acceptable business-related purchases using card:

Small tools	Seminars	Photo processing and film
Auto supplies	Office supplies	Postage
Minor equipment repairs	Printer services	Copy services
Electrical supplies	Safety supplies	Building maint. supplies
Catering	Florists	Coffee services
Hardware	Signage	

- Unacceptable uses of card (blocked):

Personal user	Cash advance	Travel & entertainment
Computer hardware	Capital purchases	Indep. contract services
Jewelry, furriers		

- All card users required to sign a purchasing card agreement stating that all use of the card will be for business purposes and within the procedures set forth.

New purchasing procedure:
1. Card user obtains approval from dept. manager for each purchase.
2. Card user contacts vendor, places orders, and provides vendor with appropriate information.
3. Goods shipped as specified and labeled "Purchasing Card" – cardholder name.
4. Goods received per standard receiving procedure with the following exception: packing list and receipt is forwarded to card user.
5. All packing lists and receipts are retained by requestors and matched against monthly statement.
6. Card user reviews statement, attaches appropriate packing lists and receipts, records JRM #'s, signs and forwards to dept. manager.
7. Dept. manager reviews statement for accuracy and initials and dates statement.
8. Dept. manager forwards to finance dept. Finance audits statement and supporting documents for compliance, sales tax, 1099.
9. Finance dept. pays from master invoice received directly from the purchasing card bank.

Controls:
- Monthly dollar limits per card
- $500 single transaction limit
- Limited number of transactions per card per day
- Merchant category blocking (i.e., cash advances, jewelry stores, appliances, etc.)

Timeline

9/3/2006	9/4–9/20	9/16–11/15	11/18–3/31	11/18–3/31	4/1–4/15	4/16–4/18	4/21–5/30	6/2/2007
Present at cb mtg.	Policy guide-lines, issuer selection, supplier enrollment	Training for Pilot: facilities, purch/fin, management	Pilot program	Concurrently revise policy and procedures	Audit, analyze 3 mo. Pilot	Report audit results	Training: company-wide	Company-wide implementation

Figure 4.7b

Cafeteria Food Service Recommendations

Background/Current Situation

- Cafeteria food service has been discontinued at TTC-AA since Jan. 1977.
- New engineering building is under construction at 1555. Planned capacity for 500.
- 1410 facility has an existing kitchen with capacity to serve 800–1000 lunches/day.
- Current 1555 lunchroom could be retrofitted to house food service (basic to full service).
- Current building renovation provides ideal time to change cafeteria setup.
- Current budget approval for 1555 renovation= $2.2 million. $1.5 million for cafeteria renovation.

Options

TTC-AA could provide one of the following options for service to employees:

Option I - Express Lane (made off campus, Served at 1555)
Option II - Satellite Service (made at 1410, Served at 1555)
Option III - Full Service (made at 1555, Served at 1555)

Legend
O = Good
△ = Fair
X = Poor

Evaluation Criteria	Option I	Option II	Option III
Hot entrees	O	O	O
Continental breakfast	X	O	O
Grilled food selection (Hamburgers, Chicken)	X	△	O
Fried food selection (Fish & Chips, French Fries)	X	△	O
Soup	O	O	O
Made to order salads & sandwiches	X	O	O
Pre-packaged salads & sandwiches	O	X	X
Perception of freshness	X	△	△
Catering prepared on site	X	O	O
Approximate annual cost of food service (varies with participation)	$85K–$101K	$90K–$195K	$97K–$150K
Approximate equipment and construction cost	$650K–$750K	$700K–$800K	$1.25–$1.5 Million

- Decision based on type of service and cost benefit TTC-AA would like to provide its employees.
- Regardless of long-term option choice, Option I service would be started immediately after vendor selection as a short-term service.
- Seating to accommodate the total of 250 employees. The area would include two sections of demountable walls which allows the eating area to be reduced to 150 capacity and create two 50 person capacity conference rooms.

Timeline

5/28/97	6/97	7/15/97	8/1/97	8/15/97	10/1/97	4/98	7/98
Present at VP meeting	Executive decision	Create bid specs.	Send out bid	Select vendor	Begin int. service	Start renovation	Target completion

Figure 4.8a   Cafeteria Food Service Recommendations example A3

To: TTC Exec. Group
From: K. Marvin
Date: 5/28/97

Comparison/Site Visits & Affiliates

	BASF	Eaton	GM Tech Ctr.	Denso	TMS	TMM-K
# of Employees	500	680	200	350	2500	7200
Type of Service	Sm. Full Serv.	Lg. Full Serv.	Express/Sat.	Sm. Full Serv.	Lg. Full Serv.	Lg. Full Serv.
% of Use	48%	95%	95%	65%	72%	88%
Lunch Hr. Range	11am–1pm	All Day	All Day	11:45–1:00	11:00–1:30	11:00 –1:30
Flex Lunch Hour	Y/30 Min.	Y/30 Min.	Y/30 Min.	No	Y/30 Min.	Yes/30 Min.
Annual $ (approx.)	$75K	$200K	$200K	$204K	$200K	$0K
Meal Cost	$3.00–$5.00	$2.00 –$3.00	$2.00–$3.00	$2.60–$5.10	$3.75–$4.95	$3.00–$4.00
Remoteness	In town many options	Very remote no options	In town many options	In town many options	In town many options	Some remote few options

Issues

Growth	• Anticipated growth to approximately 500 employees by the year 2000. At 50% participation, 250 employees would need to be served within one hour current conditions.
Flexibility	• The shorter the lunch period, the greater the participation at on-site cafeterias. • Creating range of time for lunch creates a more balanced flow of employees through the cafeteria. This promotes less time in line waiting. Would also require less space for seating.
Facilities	• Provide a full service kitchen at 1555 by complete renovation of existing lunch rooms and adjacent rooms to accommodate Option III: -Issues: Trash removal, deliveries, loss of conference room • Utilize existing 1410 kitchen with partial renovation at 1555 to accommodate Option I or II: -Issues: Movement of food out of 1410, delivery of food to 1555, paper/throw away dishes and utensils versus washable dishes and utensils

Recommendation

1) Provide for a flexible lunch hour range (ex. 11:30 am –1:30 pm), including the choice of taking only 30 minutes for lunch.
2) Recommend Option II for lunch services at TTC-AA.

Primary	-Utilizing the current 1410 facility kitchen over a full service kitchen at 1555 provides a cost savings in equipment and renovation costs. -Eliminates the need to retrofit the 1555 lunch room (an area not suited to house a full service kitchen). Wait to design a full service kitchen in the next generation of construction on the campus. -A hot meal is available with several other options for employees to obtain lunch in a reasonable time frame, including a 30-minute lunch hour.
Secondary	-Provide a pleasant environment and atmosphere for employees -Provide a professionally managed area which can function for business lunches with suppliers. -Provide an area with easy in-and-out access to avoid congestion. -Provide on-site catering to accommodate departmental lunches, business meetings, etc. -Provide off-site catering to accommodate special functions.

Figure 4.8b

The example, on the surface, may appear to differ substantially from the template previously presented, but an examination of the underlying structure suggests that it is not too dissimilar from what we described earlier in this chapter. Background and current condition information is provided, though abbreviated. Next, options are presented and evaluated systematically, both in relation to each other (in the options section) and in relation to what other companies have done (in the comparison section). Unresolved issues are outlined, and a clear recommendation is made. Finally, a high-level timeline is presented (although in the middle, not at the end). The author apparently has chosen to deviate from the suggested format because the main emphasis of the report is the analysis of alternatives and recommendation, so she made a few adaptations to the flow (moved the timeline earlier and recommendation later) and section content (providing benchmark data rather than plan details). Such adaptations are fine; in fact, they are expected. After writing a number of reports using the template as a guide, we expect you will begin to get a feel for when and how the formats can and should be modified to more effectively accomplish the desired end.

Proposal A3 Example 2

Let us take a look at another example to further illustrate how the basic outline is easily and commonly adapted to suit the intended purposes (see figure 4.9). Some readers might recognize this A3 example right away. The contents are borrowed from our good friend John Shook based on the Acme Stamping case presented in Rother and Shook's workbook *Learning to See*.[5] For those not familiar with the workbook, it introduces the main concepts of value stream mapping, or what Toyota internally calls material and information flow analysis. Even if you are not familiar with the mapping techniques in the workbook, you should be able to follow the story in this proposal A3. Those familiar with the workbook will recognize how the entire Acme Stamping example, which involves significant workplace changes, can be condensed onto a single sheet of paper. Let us look briefly at each of the major sections of the report.

The document starts off with the typical background and current condition sections, as do virtually every type of A3. The A3 then displays additional detail of the current condition in the form of a current state mapping analysis. Why? In this case, a physical transformation of a production area and significant changes to the work processes are being proposed for consideration. Even if the audience is familiar with the work processes, it is still a good idea to depict an appropriately detailed view of the existing processes in question to clarify what is and is not in the scope of the proposed change. In this case, the production process and several of the most pressing problems in the process are communicated in a highly visual and easy-to-grasp manner.

Next, the Acme Stamping A3 outlines specific goals. This section is almost always expected in problem-solving A3s but can also be found in many proposal A3s in order to make the proposal's goals clear for the audience. In addition, establishing clear objectives provides concrete criteria by which to judge success of the project. In this case, the goals section makes it clear that this is a proposal to improve lead time[6] and reduce inventory of steering brackets produced in this facility.

This particular A3 proposal then lists specific countermeasures that are being proposed in response to the problems identified in the current state depiction. The reader will probably recognize this example now as a blend of a problem-solving pattern for A3s explained in chapter 3 with a proposal A3. Often, a good proposal A3 contains sections of a problem-solving A3. After all, proposals are often solutions to specific problems.

The actual proposal, then, is depicted as a future state diagram of the new processes with the countermeasures in place. Instead of using paragraphs of text to explain the improvements, a simple chart illustrates how the improvements would work together. As in most cases, a simple picture is a more effective means of communication for explaining the nature of the proposed changes.

The A3 continues with a section making the proposed plan details clear to all affected parties. The plan includes a basic timeline, assignments, and due dates. Once the proposal is approved for implementation, it is quite likely that each party would then, in turn, create a more detailed A3 for his or her respective part of the project as needed. The final section of the A3 is a simple follow-up area that describes the need for basic checks and communication events to occur. There is no specific detail in this case, because the decision regarding implementation has not yet been reached.

This A3 is a good example of how problem solving and project work are not mutually exclusive. In both cases, the basic PDCA cycle and root-cause analysis are applicable. This sort of A3—one that uses a current state–future state pattern—is frequently used in Toyota when any sort of physical transformation, organizational change, or work-process improvement is executed because drawing current state and future state depictions help clarify the project. Thus, for organization or workplace changes, we highly recommend this pattern as a good template to follow.

These two examples illustrate how alterations to the basic proposal-writing format are possible, even desirable. It would be wonderful and simple if only one type of A3 were necessary, but this is highly impractical. Imagine if you were to expect a mechanic to fix your car using only one tool. He or she is not likely to be very productive. In reality, the world is complex and each situation is unique.

Acme Stamping Steering: Lead-time & Inventory Reduction Proposal

<u>Background</u>
- Product: stamped-steel steering brackets (left- and right-hand drive).
- 18,400 brackets/month; daily shipments in pallets of 10 trays of 20 brackets.
- Stamping division goals require reductions in lead-time and inventory of 25% this fiscal year.

<u>Current Conditions</u>
- Production Lead time: 23.6 days.
- Processing time: only 188 seconds.
- Large inventories of material between each process.
- Long changeover times; downtime in welding.

<u>Current State Analysis</u>

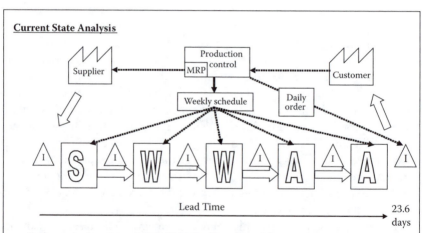

- Each process operates as isolated islands, disconnected from customer.
- Push system; material builds up between each process.
- Each process builds according to its own operating constraints (changeover, downtime, etc.)
- Plans based on 90- and 30-day forecasts from customer. Weekly schedule for each department. System is frequently overridden to make delivery.

<u>Goals</u>

Reduce lead time: 23.6 days to ≤ 5 days
Reduce inventories: Stamping -≤ 2 days
                       Welding - Eliminate
                       Shipping -≤ 2 days

Figure 4.9a   Acme Stamping example A3

To: W. Coyote
From: J. Shook
Date: 12/01/06

Countermeasures:
- Create continuous flow in through weld and assembly
- Establish takt time: Base the pace of work on customer demand
- Set new weld-assembly cell as pacemaker for entire value stream
- Establish EPE_X_ build schedule for stamping based on actual use of pacemaker cell and pull steel coils from supplier based on actual usage
- Reduce changeover time in stamping and weld
- Improve uptime in weld
- Establish material handling routes for frequent withdrawal and delivery
- Establish new production instruction system with leveling box

Proposed Future State Map

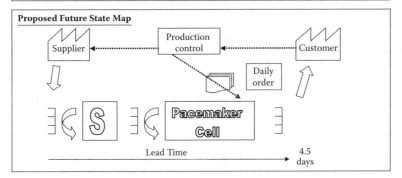

Lead Time → 4.5 days

Plan Details	1	2	3	4	5	6	7	8	9	10	11	12	Responsible	Review
CCF at pacemaker	○	△											Smith (IE)	Plt Mgr VSMgr
Kaizen each c/t to <TT														
Weld uptime to 100%	○		△											
c/o reduction to <TT	●	○	▲	▲										
Pull at pacemaker													Jones (PC)	Plt Mgr, MH Mgr VSMgr
FG = 2 days		○	▲		△									
KB		○		▲		△								
Mt'l handling				▲			△							
Leveling box				○	▲		△							
Pull from stamping													Jones (PC)	Plt Mgr MH Mgr VSMgr
WIP = 1 day						○	▲	△						
c/o < 10 min						○		△						
Pull from Supplier													Durham (Mt'l)	PC Mgr Plt Mgr VSMgr
Info flow							○	▲	△					
Daily delivery							○		▲	△				
RM = 1.5 days								○		▲	△			

Follow-up

Confirm reviews and involvement of related departments:

Confirm improvement in lead-time and inventory reduction

Roll out pilot to larger areas once completed

Figure 4.9b

Therefore, no one A3 template can frame every situation in either problem solving or proposal writing. We hope, however, that by reviewing these different examples, you will begin to get a better feel for the overall pattern and what is important to consider in each case.

Reviewing Proposal A3s

We emphasized earlier that report reviews are important for problem-solving A3s. They are even more important for proposal A3s because they typically involve decisions that affect significant numbers of people within the organization or significant amounts of money. Proposal A3s are typically reviewed on three levels. First, there is the self or peer review that should be enacted as a way to obtain some neutral feedback before venturing too far forward. This type of review helps avoid mistakes or highlight areas or alternative points of view that might not have been fully considered. Second are the alignment discussions with parties that may be affected by the proposal. They tend to be more difficult and situational in nature, depending upon the company and the nature of the contents. Third is the final report or presentation to management, who will decide whether to approve the proposal and authorize implementation. We will briefly comment on each one of these areas and some key points to consider.

Discuss with Peer Group or Advisor

Once the A3 has been drafted (or, better yet, while it is being written), it is a good idea to get some feedback from a trusted source. Just as with the A3s for problem solving, we have created a short checklist of questions to use as self-review or as a guide for obtaining feedback (see table 4.2). These are common types of questions asked during a review of an A3 proposal. The purpose of this initial review is to obtain some feedback in a careful manner for discussion. It may not be necessary in all cases, but it is often advisable, especially for less-experienced authors, before reviewing the contents with other departments.

Discuss with Affected Parties

The second stage of review is discussion with the various parties that will be affected by the proposal. No matter how brilliant and well conceived the contents might be, it is simply human nature for people to support what they have a hand in creating. An A3 that is 100 percent self-created may run into a brick wall of resistance because key individuals are not confident that their concerns have been adequately addressed in the proposal.

Table 4.2 Review Questions for Proposal A3 Reports

Background

Is there a clear theme for the report that reflects the contents?
Is the topic relevant to the organization's objectives?
Is there any other reason for working on this topic (learning purposes)?

Current condition

What information does the audience need to find my proposal compelling?
Is the current condition clear and logically depicted in a visual manner?
How could the current condition be made clearer for the audience?
Does the current condition frame the problem or situation clearly, accurately, and objectively?
Is the problem quantified in some manner or is it too qualitative?

Analysis and proposal

Is there a clear goal or target?
What specifically is to be accomplished?
How will this goal be measured or evaluated?
What will improve by how much and when?
Is the analysis detailed enough and did it probe deeply enough on the right issues?
Has cause and effect been demonstrated or linked in some manner?

Unresolved issues (optional)

What problems or constraints might exist?
What needs to be considered but cannot be resolved for the moment?
What remains to be discussed about this topic?

Implementation schedule

Are any key activities or steps missing?
Is the implementation schedule clear and reasonable?
How will the effects of implementation be verified?
How will a reflection meeting be held and when?
What budget or timing constraints exist?

Overall

Who is the audience? Does this report give them all the information necessary to make a good decision?
What personnel are affected by this proposal? Have they all been consulted?
Is the report clean, neat, and organized with good flow?
Is it readable and aesthetically pleasing?
Would I approve this proposal based only on the information contained in it?

Proposal A3s are most successful when the author communicates with or involves affected parties during the formation of the A3. Discussing one's learning and ideas with those affected by the change helps them understand the rationale for the proposed change and gives them a chance to ponder and react. At Toyota, the report author is expected to strive diligently to incorporate as much of the feedback as possible in the proposal. Even with those continuous discussions, it is fruitful to approach those individuals again with the whole picture, from diagram of the current situation and diagnosis of root cause through to implementation and follow-up plans, to ensure as much alignment as possible. It is possible that someone originally agreed to the idea in principle but is not agreeable with, for example, the timing of certain implementation steps. Thus, although the problem-solving effort may be led by an individual, the process must be carried out collaboratively with as broad an audience as is appropriate for the issue.

The Japanese use various words to describe this process, the most famous of which is probably *nemawashi*. The term consists of two words in Japanese: *ne,* meaning root, and *mawashi,* meaning to twist or rotate. The expression derives from the practice and importance of properly preparing the roots of a tree before transplanting it into the soil. The business equivalent of this practice is to dialogue with related parties in the company and lay down the proper foundations for some initial agreement or understanding about the proposal contents. There is no reason for the final meeting to be the first time affected parties hear about the proposed changes. Often this only leads to surprise, contentious debate, and tension or roadblocks. From our experience, skipping this informal yet highly important step of discussion with related parties will only lead to delays and frustrations later in the process.

A powerful thing happens, though, when using an A3 or partially completed A3 as the basis for discussions. It serves as a boundary object between parties, helping to communicate quickly and effectively the proposal, the rationale for pursuing it, details of the plan, and so forth. This is tremendously powerful in interdepartmental situations where people may speak different lingo and have different perspectives. We have seen, time and again, problems that vexed organizations for many years despite many attempts to resolve them that were speedily remedied through use of an A3 report to communicate current-state understandings and synthesize multiple viewpoints. By putting it in writing, people have something definitive that they can point to and say definitively whether they agree or not.

Obtain Approval

At Toyota, any change must receive approval before it is allowed. As mentioned in the preceding chapter, Toyota managers view the approval step as an explicit mentoring opportunity. Usually, the initial approval must be obtained by one's manager (or manager's manager). This gives the manager the opportunity to mentor the report's authors, enhance their investigative and deductive reasoning skills, help build their communication and social networking abilities, and challenge the rigor of their approach. An A3 report at Toyota is considered "approved" only when the manager endorses it by putting his or her personal stamp in red ink (or *hanko*) in the signature box. Until this seal of approval is put on the document, any third-party reader can infer that the contents have not been scrutinized or endorsed by management and are still in the formulation stage.

As part of the mentoring process, the manager also ensures that the proper process has been followed during A3 creation. Did the investigator visit the *genba* and gather enough of the right kinds of data to justify the proposed change? Does the root cause make sense? Do the countermeasures address root causes? Is the implementation plan realistic, following PDCA logic? Did they talk with the right people, and do those people support the proposal as written? Based on the responses to questions asked during review, the manager has three options: approve the proposal; reject it; or ask the author to do additional work to revise and resubmit the proposal. The most common response is to ask the writer to revise and resubmit.

Final approval in companies like Toyota does not occur until a face-to-face meeting has been held with representatives from various functions that have a say in the matter. If it is strictly an internal matter, cross-functional representation is not required. The purpose for the approval meeting is to officially decide to move forward with the proposal or to allow affected parties to air different points of view. Most of the time, with much upfront work conducted in investigation and alignment, a short meeting is all that is required and a decision can be made quickly. In more contentious cases, more joint investigation or analysis may be required. As with all companies, however, organizational leadership may have to make a decision when a compromise cannot be reached.

Your Turn

Now it is your turn again. There are endless opportunities to practice writing proposal A3s. You may already have one in mind for your specific situation. If so, we suggest that you stop here, take out a clean sheet of paper, and start to formulate your thoughts using one of the patterns we have presented. A3s are like riding a bicycle, playing golf, or learning to play a musical instrument. You will not really learn how to write and use A3s until you start trying it out yourself. The sooner you get started, the sooner you will start improving.

Part 1: Write a Proposal A3

If no specific proposal idea comes to mind, then we suggest something along the following lines. With the information provided and a little creativity based upon your own personal situation and knowledge, you should have enough information to fill out a very basic proposal A3. The important thing is for you to pick up pencil and paper and give it a try!

Imagine that you are the head of operations for a small production or service operations area within a facility. The background of the situation is that defects in the form of scrap and rework or customer complaints are increasing. Also, the current workforce has experienced a significant turnover—50 percent in the ranks of the lead people and supervisors in the past six months. A simple analysis of the situation has shown two things. First, a Pareto analysis of the defects shows that the majority of the defects or problems are caused by operations and not suppliers, product development, or process capability. You can invent your own data if necessary. Second, a further sampling of the problems by your staff has shown that most of the problems (70 to 80 percent) are fairly simple in nature to fix and should be handled by the first line of supervision in the facility, not the engineers or quality department. The remaining 20 to 30 percent of the problems are of medium to higher difficulty and should be addressed by parties outside the production work teams or supervisors. Third, a quick study of the supervisor ranks indicates that 50 percent of them have had no problem-solving training and are unfamiliar with the structured steps of basic problem solving; 40 percent of the supervisor population possess an intermediate level in problem solving; fewer than 10 percent have advanced skills in problem solving. The supervisors with the strongest problem-solving skills also have the lower problem rates in production.

Your A3 will center on proposing the implementation of a practical problem-solving training class. The options to consider might be the following: 1) You can hire a consultant who has the material developed and will put on a series of courses for $20,000; 2) the local community college has an extension course that can be taught in the evenings, on site, for $5,000 for ten weeks; and 3) you can develop your own training materials in-house, modifying some existing material, and using existing in-house talent for instructors. Ideally, you would create some sort of comparison matrix for the three examples (or others, if you can think of them) and evaluate them according to some criteria you will need to establish as well.

The example should also include the plan details for the option you favor and a clear set of deliverables as well as a timeline for the proposal implementation. If there are any unresolved issues, include them as well for discussion in the A3.

Be sure to include how you will check the effectiveness of the proposed training and how you will gauge its impact.

Part 2: Review Your A3

In appendix B, we have provided one possible proposal A3 based on the information given. At this point, the proposal should be viewed as preliminary. Now put on the hat of a reviewer, possibly a department head or supervisor who would be expected to support the problem-solving training, or the senior manager who would approve (or not!) the proposed program. Using the information and prompting questions provided earlier in this chapter, critically evaluate either your or our A3 report. We have provided our own critique in appendix B. As with the exercise in chapter 2, it is probably most beneficial to do your own critique before looking at the "answers." Again, there is no right or wrong answer as long as you are consistent with A3 thinking.

Summary

In this chapter, we have introduced a variation of the A3 report designed specifically for proposal writing. We have illustrated the flexibility of the report template through examples that show how it can be adapted to suit specific circumstances, purposes, and authors. There is no one way to write an A3, and no two A3s ever look quite the same. As you practice and understand the methods behind them, you will begin to gain some better understanding of what works and why. In chapter 5, we will show you one more derivative of the A3 that focuses on the topic of status reviews.

The important thing is not that an A3 report conforms strictly to this or that format. Rather, it is the thinking reflected in the report and the process used to create it, what we call A3 thinking. So we see in the proposal A3 a logic consistent with PDCA and a tool that serves as a mechanism to enact PDCA as a management philosophy. Furthermore, the report author is expected to synthesize information gathered through deep investigation and to present it cogently and succinctly. He or she uses the A3 report (in partial or in completed form) to help garner organizational alignment about the best course of action regarding the ideas presented. Finally, management can use the proposal A3 report to gain visibility into the processes used to develop the proposal and ensure that a systems perspective is taken in all significant decisions. Our intent in providing the templates, explanations, and examples is to give you a concrete starting point for practicing A3 thinking.

Endnotes

1 A typical purchase order process for procuring supplies or services from another company might look like this: 1) Company issues a purchase order to vendor; 2) vendor ships the material or provides the service; 3) vendor sends invoice to company; 4) company matches invoice to purchase order on record and pays vendor.

2 Alternatively, the authors could have chosen to draw a diagram depicting the existing process and show how much more simplified the process will become once purchasing cards are in use. However, the A3 authors felt that actual cost and time numbers were more important than procedural details for this audience (company vice president).

3 The proposal could be enhanced by having a comparison of competitive products (although this would be moot if all competitive products are more or less comparable) or by including some benchmark data on use of purchasing cards by other companies. However, in this case, the "approval authority" did not consider this additional information necessary for him to make a decision on the proposal.

4 See Liker, *The Toyota Way*, 239–40.

5 Mike Rother and John Shook, *Learning to See* (Brookline, MA: Lean Enterprise Institute, 1998).

6 Lead time here refers to the amount of time that transpires from when the main stock material arrives at the factory to when it is shipped to a customer. Some define lead time as the time from when a customer order is received to when it is filled.

Chapter 5

The Status A3 Report

In the preceding two chapters, we introduced the A3 tool as a summary device for problem solving and proposal writing. However, as is quickly discovered when using the tool in context, there are many shades of gray between those two types. For example, problems solved can lead to proposals to do something differently. Alternatively, proposals often solve a problem as a means to a new end state. Simply stated, problem solving and proposal writing are not always mutually exclusive. We hope, though, that presenting them as separate topics helps the reader sense the differences and possibilities of the A3 summary report, particularly their use at different points in the PDCA cycle.

We have observed a third broad category for A3s in use at Toyota that performs an equally useful though different function: the project summary or status review A3.[1] As the name implies, this type of A3 frames work that has been recently completed and succinctly summarizes it for the reader. The review might be an interim report (at the end of a pilot project or at the end of a first phase of a rollout), or it might occur at the conclusion of a project. In either case, the status A3 can be used to depict the current condition, highlight what has improved and, just as importantly, what has not improved, and begin the more important discussion of "why." As you will see in this chapter, it is also an effective capstone for the end of projects to discuss overall learning points and to key in on areas for further work or improvement.

Let us first summarize what is different about the status or project summary A3 report (or simply "status A3" for short) in comparison to the previous two types presented. After we present the chief differences, we will then walk through two examples to provide you with a better feel for the style and content.

The differences may be subtle but are important, because using the wrong type of A3 for the wrong purpose is akin to using the wrong tool for the job. Just as a hammer does not substitute well for a chisel, a status A3 is simply not appropriate until completion of at least some of the work solving a problem or implementing an approved proposal.

As noted in table 5.1, the content of a status A3 is aimed at effectively summarizing changes and results obtained in implementation. As such, it is typically used after some improvement work has been conducted on some type of problem-solving activity or proposal-related work. While ideally this verification might appear within the problem-solving or proposal style A3, it often takes another document to summarize the results more clearly and frame the next steps of discussion. Status review A3s are an excellent option to fill this need.

Table 5.1 Comparison of Different A3s

Focus	Problem solving	Proposal writing	Project status review
Thematic content or focus	Improvements related to quality, cost, delivery, safety, productivity, and so on	Policies, decisions, or projects with significant investment or implementation	Summary of changes and results as an outcome of either problem solving or proposal implementation
Tenure of person conducting the work	Novice but continuing throughout career	Experienced personnel; managers	Both novice and more experienced managers.
Analysis	Strong root-cause emphasis; quantitative/analytical	Improvement based on considering current state; mix of quantitative and qualitative	Less analysis and more focus on verification of hypothesis and action items
PDCA cycle	Documents full PDCA cycle involved in making an improvement and verifying the result	Heavy focus on the Plan step, with Check and Act steps embedded in the implementation plan	Heavy focus on the Check and Act steps, including confirmation of results and follow-up to complete the learning loop

Status A3s can be used by individuals with various levels of tenure and position within the organization. In general, the more junior the tenure of the person, the more likely the status review A3 will be used to frame more basic and local problems. With more senior persons, the status review will likely become more cross-functional and complex in nature. Analysis tends to focus on verification of prior hypotheses and action items more so than on root-cause identification or proposal merits.

Perhaps the most important difference between the status A3 and the other two types, however, is how the status A3 relates to the PDCA cycle. Specifically, the project status A3 focuses primarily on the last two parts of the PDCA cycle—the Check and Act phases—in order to verify exactly what improvements have been achieved. For problems of smaller scope, this may fit naturally within a problem-solving A3 in sufficient detail. However, for larger, more complex problems that are addressed over a longer time frame, a more detailed status review A3 is often useful, especially when management desires updates on project progress and/or a final report at the end.

Let us now take a closer look at the status A3 report to get a better understanding of the chief differences.

Storyline of the Status A3

Status A3s are of a similar size and structure as the previous two types we have discussed. The main goal of the status A3 is to present a logical snapshot of how a project or problem-solving effort is progressing, what results have been achieved, and what work still needs to be done. In general, a project or status review consists of a simple thematic statement followed by background, the current condition, the results to date, and the remaining issues and follow-up actions, as shown in figure 5.1. There are, of course, derivatives of this style, and we will comment on those differences where applicable. For starters, though, we will stick to the most basic formula for explanation.

Theme

As with the other types of A3s, the status A3 report still begins with a thematic title that introduces the content to the audience. The theme should objectively describe the content addressed in the report, while clearly indicating that it is a summary or status report. As an initial example, we will describe the A3 entitled "Corporate Credit Card Implementation Status," which is related to the proposal A3 report with a similar title in the preceding chapter.

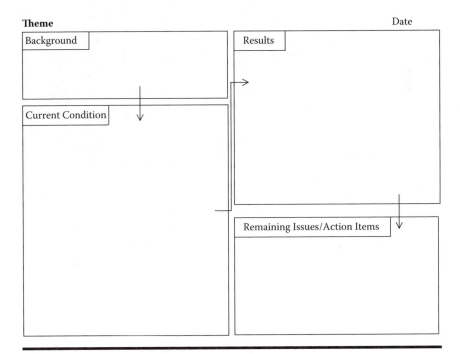

Figure 5.1   Typical flow of the project status review A3 report

Background

The status A3 report begins by summarizing the pertinent background information for the reader to digest. As always, the content of the background section depends heavily upon the audience. An internal group familiar with the project may not need as much detail about the situation, whereas an audience less familiar with the project may need the highlights of a prior proposal A3 summarized to provide sufficient contextual information to understand the content.

In the example illustrated in figure 5.2, the background section assumes a fair amount of familiarity with the project, because it was also covered in the preceding chapter. It serves primarily as a reminder, pointing out that the project is aimed at implementing a corporate credit card system to be used on all purchases equal to and under $500 and is expected to result in cost and time savings. The author has also included a high-level overview of the implementation strategy.

Here are some key points to keep in mind about any background section for an A3:

■ Make the overall context of the situation as clear as possible.

- Implementing purchasing credit cards for purchases < $500 is expected to bring significant time and cost savings.
- Purchases < $500 account for 47% of all purchases, but only 5% of total dollar outlay.
- A new procedure and controls were needed.

Implementation strategy:
- Select card issuer.
- Establish policies and controls.
- Conduct training for card users in the facilities, purchasing, and finance departments.
- Conduct pilot program in same departments.

Figure 5.2   Example of background section of a project status review A3

- Identify the target audience and write accordingly.
- Provide the necessary information that the audience needs to know before going forward.
- Explain how this topic aligns with company goals.
- Include any other information, such as historical data, dates, or names, that might help the audience understand the importance of this problem.

Current Condition

Just as with problem-solving and proposal A3s, the background section of a status A3 is followed by a current condition section. The current condition in this A3 is a bit different, however, from the previous ones discussed. In the A3s previously discussed, the current condition sections described the original state of the process or situation. In a status A3, though, change or transformation should have already occurred. So the current condition described in the status A3 is the new state or a summary of the changes that have been made. Ideally, the old future state or condition has now become the current state.

As illustrated in figure 5.3, some type of Gantt chart can be used to represent the set of activities that have been implemented over a period of time. In the Corporate Credit Card Implementation Status example, this is suitable, because the changes are relatively invisible to the naked eye of the observer. The differences in work processing are mainly administrative in nature and difficult to depict with process or flow charts. When applicable, however, we recommend presenting a visual image of the transformation that has occurred to the process. We illustrate this approach with a second example later in the chapter.

In the Corporate Credit Card Implementation Status report, the report author has made visible for the audience all the main steps taken during the implementation phase. In addition to the progress timelines, an evaluation column summarizes how well the implementation has gone with respect to simple

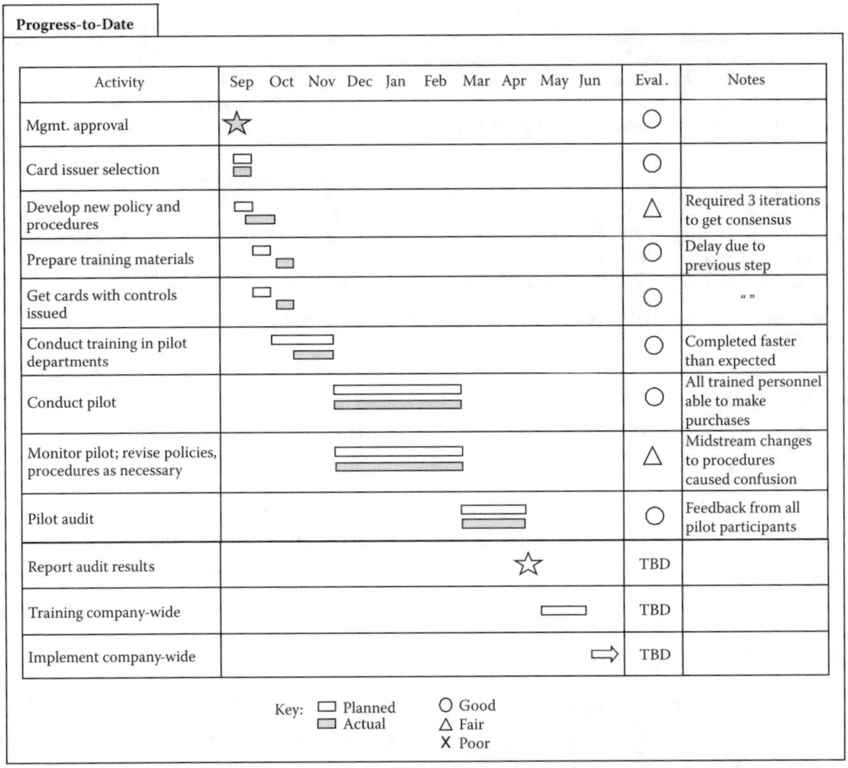

Progress-to-Date

Activity	Sep Oct Nov Dec Jan Feb Mar Apr May Jun	Eval.	Notes
Mgmt. approval	☆	O	
Card issuer selection	▤	O	
Develop new policy and procedures	▭▭	△	Required 3 iterations to get consensus
Prepare training materials	▭▭	O	Delay due to previous step
Get cards with controls issued	▭▭	O	" "
Conduct training in pilot departments	▭▭	O	Completed faster than expected
Conduct pilot	▭▭	O	All trained personnel able to make purchases
Monitor pilot; revise policies, procedures as necessary	▭▭	△	Midstream changes to procedures caused confusion
Pilot audit	▭▭	O	Feedback from all pilot participants
Report audit results	☆	TBD	
Training company-wide	▭	TBD	
Implement company-wide	⇨	TBD	

Key: ▭ Planned   O Good
       ▭ Actual   △ Fair
                   X Poor

Figure 5.3   Example of current condition section of a project status review A3

criteria. Glancing down this column, the reader can quickly discern that the implementation has proceeded generally well and on time with only a couple of major tasks remaining. One of the tasks is the report of the results, which this A3 outlines.

Here are some key points to keep in mind when writing the current condition section of a status review A3:

■ Clearly depict an overview of the current condition in a visual manner. If possible, show the before and after states for clarity.
■ When the current condition has not significantly changed, outline the work that has been performed with respect to timelines and objectives.
■ As much as possible, use quantitative measures to depict the status of the current state, not just qualitative opinions or bulleted points.
■ If additional supporting material is needed, use additional handouts to supplement the material in the A3.

Results

The most important section of the status review A3 is the results section. The purpose of the document, after all, is to provide the reader with a summary of the impact that the initiatives or action items have had. It is the true Check part of the PDCA phase. The goal of this section is to convey quantitatively the impact that has been achieved so far in the project. The metrics used should reflect the ones most important for judging the success of the project.

The statement often used in basic science and problem solving, "standards are a basis for comparison," very much applies to changes and improvements within organizations. In fact, within Toyota circles, one commonly hears comments that without a standard and basis for comparison, there is no *kaizen* (or improvement). In other words, how do we know if a process or system has improved unless we actually take time to measure and compare before and after results objectively? Thus, the results section of a status A3 should be an objective and unbiased presentation of the results from the improvement actions. The goal is not to show just what is better but to show in a balanced fashion whether the result is really a net improvement. Oftentimes, this means showing more than one metric, such as quality, cost, and timing.

In figure 5.4, the Corporate Credit Card Implementation Status A3 displays three metrics and a user survey. The results section shows that, as predicted, both cost and time dimensions have improved considerably using the new card

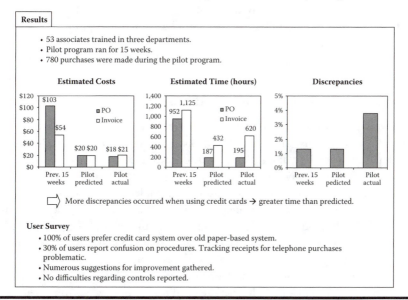

Figure 5.4   Example of results for a project status review A3

system, although time has not improved as much as expected. Somewhat unexpectedly, discrepancies increased in reconciling statements, which partially explains why time did not improve as much as expected. As a follow-up assignment, more work will be needed in this area to improve upon this unanticipated problem. Note that even in this potentially nebulous policy change, the report author employs quantitative metrics to demonstrate and verify actual improvement.

As an additional results item, a simple survey of users was conducted as well. Some things like "preference" or "ease of use" are not always captured in measurement systems. In these cases, it is advisable to include a simple survey of opinions, which can be as easy as asking users whether they prefer the system and then tabulating the responses. A more sophisticated evaluation might ask several questions that can be scored on a scale of 1 (low) to 5 (high), for example. The key point, however, remains: to verify by use of an objective standard whether the condition has improved.

Here are some points to keep in mind for creating the results section of the status A3:

- Use metrics that are the most important for evaluating progress.
- Make sure the metrics are objective and quantified, not just subjective opinions.
- Present a balanced set of metrics to show that an improvement in one area has not been offset in another.
- Make sure the metrics are an accurate basis for comparison and not just convenient points of data.
- Strive to show what has and, just as importantly, what has not improved.

Unresolved Issues/Follow-up Actions

The concluding section of a typical status A3 report is a set of unresolved issues and follow-up actions. This section may contain a variety of different pieces of information depending upon the outcome of the project results. We will outline some of the most common items and mention some other patterns as well.

In figure 5.5 for the Corporate Credit Card Implementation Status example, the follow-up actions section is organized around the five remaining tasks that need to be performed to complete the pilot study and pilot-study review. Organizing the tasks in a tabular fashion is an entirely appropriate way of organizing and summarizing the remaining work for this example. Imagine, however, if the implementation results had not gone so well. What if the estimated cost and time savings were far less than predicted? In such cases (which unfortunately do occur), the answer is to return to problem-solving mode and consider "why"

Remaining Issues/Future Actions		
Activity	**Status**	**Responsibility**
Revise procedures	Completed	Purchasing
User and managerial review of revised procedures	In-progress (complete by 4/21)	Purchasing
Review and revise training	In-progress (complete by 4/30)	Purchasing
Company-wide training	To start 5/1	Training Dept.
Full company implementation	To start 6/2	Purchasing

Figure 5.5   Example of remaining issues/follow-up actions section for a project status review A3 report

the results were not achieved. Until the root cause for the shortcoming is identified, it is pointless to attempt to go forward. The follow-up section, then, may outline further tests or pilot trials, or it may identify specific countermeasures for discussion with the audience. Thus, the contents placed in the concluding section of the report depend heavily upon the results in the Check phase of the implementation project. Think of this section as the Act part of the PDCA cycle, outlining what should be done to complete the improvement cycle.

Here are some key points to keep in mind when drafting the final section for a status A3:

- Highlight what actions items still need to be completed to finish the project.
- If some results are not in line with expectations, ask why and detail either the next set of steps to get to the root cause or the potential countermeasures for discussion.
- Consider what roadblocks or unresolved issues might still exist and what work needs to be done with respect to those items.
- Consider whether any other stakeholders may be affected in some manner that will need to be addressed.
- Consider unresolved issues related to budget, training, and shifts in responsibility.

Total Effect

Overall, the main purpose of this type of A3 is to present the status of work in progress. Starting with the report theme, the author should strive to provide the pertinent background information for the audience and depict the new vcurrent situation (either of the process/system being studied or the project itself) as factually and as visually as possible. The most critical aspect of the status review A3, however, is to present whether the anticipated improvements have been observed. Thoughtful use of charts, metrics, surveys, and so on create the basis for a rigorous assessment of project results. The report concludes with a list of appropriate follow-up actions, some of which may already be in progress.

Corporate Credit Card Implementation Status

Background

- Implementing purchasing credit cards for purchases < $500 is expected to bring significant time and cost savings.
- Purchases < $500 account for 47% of all purchases, but only 5% of total dollar outlay.
- A new procedure and controls were needed.

Implementation strategy:
- Select card issuer.
- Establish policies and controls.
- Conduct training for card users in the facilities, purchasing, and finance departments.
- Conduct pilot program in same departments.

Progress-to-Date

Activity	Sep Oct Nov Dec Jan Feb Mar Apr May Jun	Eval.	Notes
Mgmt. approval	☆	O	
Card issuer selection	▭	O	
Develop new policy and procedures		△	Required 3 iterations to get consensus
Prepare training materials		O	Delay due to previous step
Get cards with controls issued		O	" "
Conduct training in pilot departments		O	Completed faster than expected
Conduct pilot		O	All trained personnel able to make purchases
Monitor pilot; revise policies, procedures as necessary		△	Midstream changes to procedures caused confusion
Pilot audit		O	Feedback from all pilot participants
Report audit results	☆	TBD	
Training company-wide		TBD	
Implement company-wide	⇨	TBD	

Key: ▭ Planned   O Good
     ▬ Actual   △ Fair
                 X Poor

Figure 5.6a   Corporate Credit Card Implementation Status example status A3 report

Figure 5.6 depicts the completed A3 report for the Corporate Credit Card Implementation Status example. There are, of course, other ways the report could have been written. The important thing is that the author has engaged in A3 thinking and has written a status review that is coherent and organized, and flows well from beginning to end in a way that is consistent with PDCA management. The work is not yet finished, but after a discussion with pertinent parties, the remaining items can be conducted in an efficient manner. In order to illustrate the adaptability of the A3 tool, we will present one more status review A3 report for comparison.

To: J. Griffin, VP Admin.
From: Finance & Purchasing
Date: 4/12/2007

Results

- 53 associates trained in three departments.
- Pilot program ran for 15 weeks.
- 780 purchases were made during the pilot program.

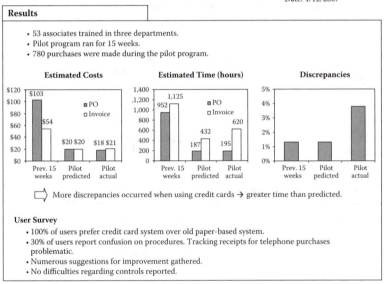

More discrepancies occurred when using credit cards → greater time than predicted.

User Survey

- 100% of users prefer credit card system over old paper-based system.
- 30% of users report confusion on procedures. Tracking receipts for telephone purchases problematic.
- Numerous suggestions for improvement gathered.
- No difficulties regarding controls reported.

Remaining Issues/Future Actions

Activity	Status	Responsibility
Revise procedures	Completed	Purchasing
User and managerial review of revised procedures	In-progress (complete by 4/21)	Purchasing
Review and revise training	In-progress (complete by 4/30)	Purchasing
Company-wide training	To start 5/1	Training Dept.
Full company implementation	To start 6/2	Purchasing

Figure 5.6b

Status A3 Example

Figure 5.7 displays a status A3 based on the Acme Stamping example from chapter 4. The original proposal used the current state–future state style to propose some physical transformation changes on the shop floor (refer to figure 4.9). Once the proposal has been approved and the implementation plan executed, it

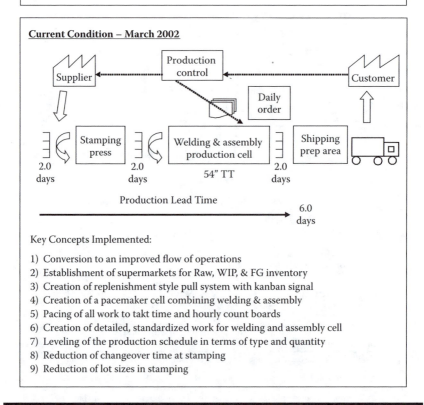

Background

- Stamping division goals require reductions in lead-time, and inventory of 25% this fiscal year.
- Bracket value stream was a push style of operations with long lead-time, excess inventory, over-production, and poor on-time delivery performance.
- A project was initiated to improve in these dimensions, targeting full completion by June 2002.

Current Condition – March 2002

Production control

Supplier

Customer

Daily order

Stamping press   Welding & assembly production cell   Shipping prep area

2.0 days   2.0 days   54" TT   2.0 days

Production Lead Time   6.0 days

Key Concepts Implemented:

1) Conversion to an improved flow of operations
2) Establishment of supermarkets for Raw, WIP, & FG inventory
3) Creation of replenishment style pull system with kanban signal
4) Creation of a pacemaker cell combining welding & assembly
5) Pacing of all work to takt time and hourly count boards
6) Creation of detailed, standardized work for welding and assembly cell
7) Leveling of the production schedule in terms of type and quantity
8) Reduction of changeover time at stamping
9) Reduction of lot sizes in stamping

Figure 5.7a   Lead Time and Inventory Reduction Project Status Review example status A3 report

is logical to stop and ask whether the situation improved or not. In such cases, a status A3 is a great way to present the answer to this question.

To: W. Coyote
From: J. Shook
Date: 03/06/02

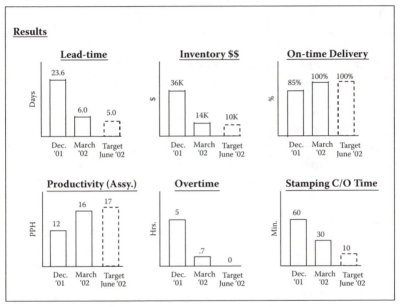

Remaining Issues/Action Items

Category	Remaining Problem	Counter-measure	Responsibility & Due Date
Lead-time	.5 days over goal	Reduce stamping WIP	PC by 5/30
Inventory	$4K over goal	Purchase parts market	PC by 5/30
Delivery	N/A	Maintain performance	Operations
Productivity	1 PPH under goal	Eliminate overtime	Ops. by 5/30
Overtime	.7 hours over goal	Eliminate minor stops	Maint. by 5/30
C/O Time	20 min. over goal	Reduce internal work	Eng. by 5/30

Figure 5.7b

The follow-on status A3 (figure 5.7) begins with a standard background section and description of relevant information. Much like the preceding example, this is a simple bullet-point summary to help the audience recall the context of the situation.

The current condition section, however, is quite different from the preceding example. This case involves a physical transformation of the production process. In the proposal A3, the author presented a current state examination followed by a proposed future state to consider for approval. At this point in time, however, the "current" conditions resemble the "future state" conditions in the proposal A3, with whatever changes transpired in implementation. So the report author depicts the process changes by inserting a graphic that represents how the improved process currently works. The key items implemented are also listed for reader convenience.[2]

The results sections is the critical part of the status A3, as we finally see quantitatively whether improvement has occurred. In this case, the project was evaluated on the basis of six operational metrics: lead time, inventory, on-time delivery, productivity, overtime, and changeover time on the stamping press. Other cases may involve fewer metrics or may include financial as well as operational metrics. In this example, only one of the set goals has actually been attained so far, although the other ones are close.

In instances such as this, where more work needs to be done to attain the desired goals, the logical next step is to return to problem-solving mode and ask the fundamental question "why" and start to probe for root causes again. The five-whys analysis, however, is often not shown in this section, because this is a status review A3. If the problems and discrepancies are large enough, the area not meeting a goal might be a good candidate for a more detailed problem-solving A3 exercise. For this status A3, the author decided to summarize the remaining areas for work and identify them as remaining problems to be solved with initial hypotheses on countermeasures, due dates, and responsibilities for further discussion at the time of presentation.

Discuss with a Peer Group or Advisor

As with all A3s, report authors should discuss their status A3 reports with peers or advisors as it is being drafted. It is always useful to practice a presentation before actually giving it for the first time. We have created a short checklist of questions to use as self-review or as a guide for obtaining feedback (see table 5.2). These are common types of questions asked during a review of a status A3 report. We suggest reflecting upon the questions and preparing to answer related topics as necessary.

Table 5.2 Review Questions for Project Status Review A3 Reports

Background

Is the theme of the project clearly stated?

Does the project relate to the goals of the company?

Is the reason why the project was undertaken clear?

What other information might be useful for the audience?

Current condition

Is the current condition clear and logically depicted in a visual manner?

Does it clearly show what progress been made or what specific action has been taken?

Does the current condition frame the problem or situation clearly, accurately, and objectively?

Is the current condition quantified in some manner or is it too qualitative?

Results

What results have been obtained in the project so far?

Are the results clearly indicated and quantified in some manner?

Has improvement actually taken place?

Are these the right metrics to show that improvement has been made?

What else might explain the change in the metrics?

Have any areas been adversely affected by the change(s)?

For areas where the improvement is not as great as expected, is it clear why or why not?

Unresolved issues/follow-up action items

What remaining problems exist in the project?

What needs to be done to achieve progress as planned?

What other items need to be conducted to sustain the gains and ensure success?

Who else needs to know about this result?

Your Turn

Now it is your turn. There are endless opportunities to practice writing an A3 status report. You might already have one in mind for your specific situation based upon work you are currently completing. If so, we suggest you stop, take out a clean sheet of paper, and start to formulate your thoughts using one of the patterns just presented. Alternatively, use the problem-solving exercise you completed earlier to outline a hypothetical status review A3. Anticipate how the project may play out and what results you might see, and then experiment with how you could communicate them in a status A3 report.

Summary

In this chapter, we have introduced a variation of the A3 report designed specifically for conducting status reviews. We have illustrated the flexibility of the report template through examples that show how it can be adapted to suit specific circumstances, purposes, and authors. There is no one way to write an A3, and no two reports ever look quite the same. As you practice and understand the methods behind them, you will begin to gain some better understanding of what works and why, based upon experience. Other derivatives of the format and style are possible, and we encourage you to experiment with them as well. However, the majority of the time, we find it a good practice to start with the template used in the examples provided.

A key point in all cases is to reflect upon the main points we have mentioned in each chapter and to keep in mind the fundamental elements of good PDCA management along with proper communication.

Endnotes

1 Internally, within Toyota, reports alternatively called "project reviews," "progress reviews," "implementation reviews," "results reviews," nonproject "status reviews," and even "project status reviews" would all fall within this category. The categorization of A3 reports we have employed in this book is derived from the training materials of Toyota's U.S.-based engineering group but is not necessarily accepted corporate-wide.

2 Often on certain topics there is a certain amount of inevitable jargon that is used for communication, for example, the terms "kanban," "pull system," and "takt time," used in the example A3. For readers unfamiliar with these terms, kanban is a Japanese word used to indicate a signal-based method for initiating production. A pull system is a type of production control that relies upon replenishment of inventory rather than building to a forecast. Takt time refers to establishing a pace for production work based upon average demand as defined by the customer. In general, we suggest trying to keep the use of jargon to a minimum unless you are presenting to an audience that is as familiar with your language as you are.

Chapter 6

Notes on Form and Style

In the preceding three chapters, we presented examples of different styles of A3s for the purposes of problem solving, proposal writing, and reporting project status. The styles represent variations on the theme of what we term A3 thinking, derived from common patterns of use we have observed in practice at Toyota. The example reports can serve as generic starting points for writing your own A3s. The discussion thus far has focused primarily on content. In this chapter, we shift focus to the form and style of A3 report writing.

Regardless of what flavor of report one writes, the mechanics of form, style, and use of graphics remain essentially the same. We have assumed the traditional perspective that A3 reports are pencil-and-paper forms, which is still the preferred method of learning to write A3 reports within Toyota, because the thought process and skill development are more important than expediency. The space and size constraints imposed by the pencil-and-paper approach tend to force A3 thinking more rigorously yet provide more flexibility relative to computer technologies, because the writer can focus on what to communicate rather than on how to make the machine do what the writer wants it to do. We will address computerization in chapter 7.

At Toyota, form and style are as important as the content of an A3 report. The reason is simple: Form and style can significantly affect the communication efficacy of the report. Over years of use and evolution at Toyota, A3 reports have developed their own form and style conventions to maximize the information density and communication effectiveness of the written reports. We will now review the key form and style points for A3 report writing.

Form

A3 reports are so named because they fit on one side of an A3-sized sheet of paper, roughly equivalent to an 11 x 17-inch sheet. The flow of the report is top-to-bottom on the left side, then top-to-bottom on the right side (refer to figures 3.1, 4.1, and 5.1). Reports are written in sections, usually starting with a theme or issue statement. Each section is clearly labeled, arranged in a logical flow, and separated from other sections by being enclosed in a box with ample margins between boxes.

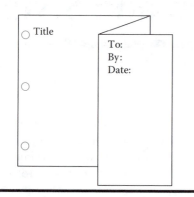

Figure 6.1   A3 trifold

The title of the report should be placed at the top left, so that when the report is trifolded (as in figure 6.1) for storage in a three-ring binder, the title is clearly visible. The title should unambiguously indicate the subject and purpose of the report. The author should place the name of the recipient ("To:"), author byline ("From:"), and date in the top (or bottom) right corner. This way, the author, date, and recipient are also clearly visible after the sheet is trifolded. The recipient, generally speaking, is the approval authority mentioned in chapter 2.

Reports should be neat, well organized, and aesthetically pleasing so that the form of the report aids rather than hinders the communication of the report's contents. Generally speaking, this means making ample use of white space, achieving good use of symmetry, lining up box edges, and aligning the leading edges of headings, paragraphs, and lists. Reports should leave enough space on the far left for a three-hole punch.

Readability is the overriding principle. Using the same text styles and sizes throughout (such as one for headings and one for body text) greatly aids readability. Text size should not be too small, which generally means a font size of 10 or greater, and not too fancy. Headings should be clearly distinguishable from body text.

Style

Perhaps the most salient characteristic of A3 reports is their brevity. A readable text size combined with the space constraint of fitting all the important information on one sheet of paper necessitates an extremely brief report. As such, there is no room for repetition, superfluous information, or extra words. Writing must be direct and brief.

A3 report writing has developed its own style, which is heavy on the use of bulleted and numbered lists, with little, if any, use of the paragraph form. The reason for this is simple: Although it may not earn any literary awards, breaking the key points into a set of succinct bulleted items encourages the author to both identify the key points he or she wants to make, and state them clearly and concisely. Consider the following example:

> In the current state of our 5S program, we do not seem to have clear ownership and accountability of an area, since an area could be cleaned by any number of associates, and assignments are not clear. In fact, specific assignments are not made. As a result, the work area is in disarray with dust buildup, missing and broken shelf dividers and face plates, missing supplies, and general disorganization.

The reader gets the general gist of what the author is trying to convey, but the particular points are muddled, and the reader must make the effort to pull them out. The same information can be communicated more effectively as follows:

Current condition:

1. 5S assignments are not clear.
2. Area ownership has not been established.
3. Work area is messy:
    a. Dust buildup on shelves
    b. Missing/broken shelf dividers and face plates
    c. Supplies missing and disorganized

In the second example, the main points are unmistakable, and the particular data describing the specifics of a messy work area are clearly connected to that point. Note also the use of white space between each numbered/bulleted item in the example to improve readability.

Lists should maintain a parallel grammatical structure, so, if the first item begins with a verb, the rest of the items in the list should begin with a verb in the same tense. Numbering lists can make items easier to reference in discussion (for example, "Referring to the second bullet under item #3 in the Current Condition").

Experienced A3 report authors tend to have a strong preference for active voice over passive voice. Consider the following pair of statements:

- The goals are set by the manager.
- The manager sets the goals.

Both statements convey the same information, but the second statement does so more concisely. The first is passive voice whereas the second is active voice, meaning the subject performs the action. Interestingly, we tend to use active voice in day-to-day conversation more so than passive voice, so the flow is more natural. In addition, heavy reliance on passive voice can quickly devolve into long, wordy, and complex statements. Brevity, conciseness, and directness are the preferred writing style for A3 reports.

In addition to being clear and brief, authors should write as specifically as possible. Rather than write that the number of errors must decrease in order to achieve the target, for example, it would be more specific to say that the number of errors must decrease from the current average of eight per month to two per month or fewer.

A3 authors within Toyota often highlight key points in the text by underlining or boldfacing them. This way, the astute reader can grasp the essence of the report by simply skimming the highlighted information. Report authors should be consistent in their use of highlighting and take care not to overuse it.

As with all forms of technical writing, proper use of grammar and spelling should always be a priority. These can significantly affect the readability, and in some cases the actual meaning, of what is written. Consider the following example:

The goals of the project are to improve quality service costs and delivery.

The goals of the project are to improve quality, service costs, and delivery.

The goals of the project are to improve quality, service, costs, and delivery.

The addition of commas at appropriate places changes the meaning of the statement, successively, from two metrics to three metrics to four. Because this would have significant implications for later sections of the A3 report, proper punctuation to convey the most accurate meaning becomes critical.

Finally, A3 report authors should always write to an audience. This means the authors should have a good understanding of what the audience already knows and what the audience wants or needs to know, and then must craft the report to get the message across swiftly and effectively. It also means that the author should avoid jargon and terminology that may be unfamiliar to the audience; and if such terms are unavoidable, the author must define them.

Graphics

Well-designed graphics can communicate complex ideas with clarity, precision, and efficiency, particularly in dealing with quantitative data. The advent of digital-imaging technology has made it possible to incorporate images from actual hardware or job-site environments. When designed and used properly, graphics can powerfully communicate a message. However, when used improperly, graphics can become confusing or non-value-added, so we endeavor in this section to provide a handful of guidelines for the design and use of graphics in A3 reports.[1]

Understand Your Data

The first rule in the use of graphics is to have a clear idea of the message. With the objective in mind, the report author chooses the data and graphical type most appropriate for that objective. To choose the right data to present, one should consider whether the absolute or relative values are most important, for example, number of sales calls versus number of sales calls per salesperson.

How much data to present can be an important consideration, particularly in looking at trend data. Does the trend over the past couple of months portray an accurate picture, or should the trend of the past year or two years be included? Next, would it be best to show individual data points or summary data such as averages, standard deviations, proportions, or moving averages? The A3 report author must exercise a good deal of discernment in selecting the data to present.

Use the Best Graph for the Data

In presenting the data, the author has many options. Table 6.1 lists the most common graph types and their suitability in displaying certain kinds of information. Again, the author must choose the most appropriate graph type for the situation, taking into consideration both the objective (or message) that the graph is communicating and the nature of the data involved.

Label Properly

To create clear, useful, and visually appealing graphs, authors would be wise to follow a few simple guidelines. First, every graph should have a title or caption

Table 6.1 Common Graph Types

Type of graph	Applicability
Line graph	Showing trends over time; comparing multiple data sets over time

Line Chart

Pie chart	Displaying the breakdown or percentage of a whole

Pie Chart

Bar chart (vertical or horizontal)	Comparing categories of data along a single dimension

Bar Chart

Pareto chart	Focusing attention on the largest problem areas

Pareto Chart

Stacked bar chart *(absolute or percentage)*	Showing relative change of both total quantity and percentage breakdown across categories

Stacked Bar Chart

Histogram	Depicting the distribution, variation, or spread of the data; showing the deviation from standard

Histogram

Scatter plot	Illustrating the relationship between two variables (such as cause and effect)

Scatter Plot

Flow chart	Summarizing the steps involved in a process and their relationships

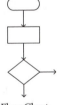

Flow Chart

that clearly and concisely states the main point of the graph. Second, labels are critical for vertical and horizontal axes, and for any data categories. Graphs without labels are often rendered useless. Third, choose an appropriate scale for the data. The choice of scale can dramatically affect the perceived significance of a feature or trend in the data.

Use as Little Ink as Possible

Edward Tufte[2] further recommends that charts and graphs use the minimum amount of ink possible. This has the effect of cleaning up the visual clutter so that the focus is on the data rather than on the design of the graph, and the main point(s) more clearly stand out. Incidentally, the default settings of most standard graphics programs (such as Microsoft Excel) produce a great deal of visual clutter. The implications of removing ink include the following:

- Minimizing redundancy (for example, do not use two lines when one line will do)
- Eliminating cross-hatching
- Replacing legends with labels directly on the data presented
- Avoiding use of 3D bars
- Removing gridlines; if they are necessary, replacing them with a white grid

Figure 6.2 illustrates the difference between graphs that do and do not conform to Tufte's guidelines. In the top chart, we can see redundancy in the chart title and vertical axis label, in the many zeros used in the vertical axis scale numbering and in the legend. These are eliminated in the bottom chart. Furthermore, since the trend is of interest more so than individual data points, the data points can be eliminated. Also note that the Excel default of slanting the horizontal axis labels leads to readability problems, which are corrected in the bottom chart. Finally, tick marks, chart border, and horizontal gridlines were replaced with a white grid. The effect is a cleaner, more compact graph that more immediately conveys the production volume trends in 2006.

Let the Graphic Talk

In A3 reports, if something can be communicated graphically, it should be. But given the paucity of space in an A3 report, redundancy with the text should generally be avoided; simply let the graphic tell the story on its own. As a final note, it is generally a good idea to note the data source.

Tables

Tables are also a useful way to organize and communicate a complex set of ideas or data efficiently. The general guidelines for tables are similar to those for the use of graphics: Keep it simple, avoid visual clutter, and make the data

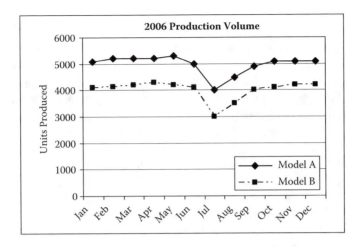

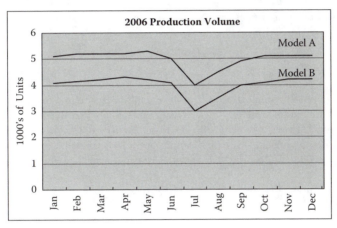

Figure 6.2   Comparison of graph designs

(and therefore the message) stand out. We have found that eliminating all vertical rules and using the minimum number of horizontal rules necessary creates a clean, aesthetically appealing table that is easy to read. An example is shown in figure 6.3.

	Alternatives		
	A	B	C
Speed	△	✕	○
Accuracy	○	△	○
Cost	○	✕	○
Weight	✕	○	△

Figure 6.3   Example table

Summary

A3 reports are clearly written and concise. One of the challenges in writing A3 reports is synthesizing and distilling a lot of information down into its salient points, and then communicating those points clearly and persuasively. But the clarity and precision resulting from this kind of thinking is one of the real values of A3 reports and is what helps enhance problem-solving and decision-making capability within an organization. It is often easy to write a very concise report that leaves out key information. It is also easy (though perhaps not quite as easy) to write a long report that contains all potentially relevant information without making a clear point. Distilling all the information about a complex issue down to the most salient points and then crafting a way to communicate it concisely and effectively is hard work! It requires the author to think deeply about what the message is, what is critical for the audience to know in order to act on the information, and, conversely, what is not critical and can be left to supporting documentation. But the rewards are worth the effort.

Endnotes

1 For a more thorough treatment of data graphics and related topics, see R. Harris, Information Graphics—A Comprehensive Illustrated Reference (New York: Oxford University Press, 1999); E. Tufte, Envisioning Information (Cheshire, CT: Graphics Press, 1990); G. Zelansky, Say It with Charts (New York: McGraw-Hill, 2005); G. Zelansky, Say It with Presentations (New York: McGraw-Hill, 2000).

2 E. R. Tufte, The Visual Display of Quantitative Information (Cheshire, CT: Graphics Press, 1983).

Chapter 7

Supporting Structures

To this point, we have discussed at length the rigorous problem-solving approaches and efficient communication promoted by widespread adoption of A3 reports, what we call A3 thinking. We then introduced the basic content and mechanics of A3 report writing, along with examples and points of guidance in writing three basic types of A3 reports, with variations. We now turn our attention to a number of broader issues that, in our study and personal experience in working with A3 documents in Japan and the United States, are important to the creation of an A3 report system.

Writing an A3 report as an individual is a fairly simple thing to do. And an individual can improve personal effectiveness by regularly writing and communicating with A3 reports. But to harness the full potential of the tool, the A3 report should be implemented on an organization-wide basis, that is, as part of an A3 report system. This is because an increase in organizational (not simply individual) knowledge, skill, and lateral networks generates faster response times, fewer errors, higher quality, and better overall problem-solving capability, all with little additional cost. The goal is not simply to implement a new management tool or program that will help the organization make incremental improvements; rather, it is to develop a flexible system that simultaneously develops people's skills and know-how, addresses problems that in some way are hindering the organization from surpassing its goals, and captures and disseminates the learning gained from problem-solving activity. The beauty of the A3 report is that, when implemented properly, this one tool can be used to accomplish all of these aims, with dramatic effects.

As we work with early adopters, the same support structure issues seem to surface repeatedly: development of standard templates; scope control; handwritten versus computer-generated reports; storage of completed documents; and coaching and approval systems. We expect many readers likely have the same questions as they think about creating an organizational improvement system based on the A3 report. So, in this chapter, we discuss each of these issues at some length and relate what we have learned and observed that affects the overall success of utilizing A3 reports. Thinking through these points and addressing them in the context of your own situation can help your improvement journey using A3 reports go more smoothly.

Standard Templates

Inevitably, one of first issues that organizations think they must tackle in designing an A3 report system is the development of standard templates. So we often get the question, "Is there a single best way to write A3 reports?" The answer from our experience and findings is "No." Do not try to force a square peg into a round hole. For ease in learning and reference, we have outlined three basic types of A3 reports in the preceding chapters, which can be seen as templates. The truth is, however, that if you visit Toyota and ask to see 100 A3s, you would be astounded by the diversity of report formats. Every report is uniquely designed for the specific problem, issue, and purpose of its author. In fact, within Toyota, there is only general agreement that there are three basic types of A3s!

Does this mean that there are no standards or set of basic beliefs governing the use of A3s in Toyota? Again, the answer is "No." There are plenty of basic standards and beliefs governing the usage of A3 reports, which we have highlighted in the preceding chapters. The confusion may stem in part from the meaning of the word "standard" in English versus its usage in Toyota. In most English-language dictionaries, the word standard implies "a rule" or "a prescribed way of doing things." In many operations, standards take on an even more narrow definition and often imply a strict sequence of steps that must be completed within a specified time period. The sentence "We have a standard way of doing things" implies that everyone should always follow the prescribed method and never deviate.

In Toyota, however, the meaning and intent of the word "standard" is closer to another definition, a "basis for comparison." In other words, it is more of a scientific definition as used in experimental research. A standard is necessary in order to determine whether an improvement has been achieved. If the standard shows that yield has changed (say, from 85 percent to 95 percent), then it is possible to state with some degree of confidence that improvement has occurred. If the standard shows no change, then improvement has not truly occurred.

In practice, A3 reports are similar to this latter notion of standard. The key point is to use A3 reports to summarize, present, propose, or analyze daily work routines and processes following a PDCA cycle. The goal is not to write A3 reports with perfect lines and boxes or adhere to one way of writing reports (a standard way of doing things). Rather, the goal is to improve using a structured approach, to document the basic approach and results in a manner consistent with company values and practices, and to communicate that approach to the appropriate audience effectively. Thus, the A3 templates serve more as a basis for evaluation (asking whether the basic storyline is clear and whether it has the essential pieces) more so than a strict report outline that must be followed. In the broadest sense, the only things standard about A3 reports is that they fit into a structured PDCA pattern and begin with a blank A3-sized sheet of paper.

Does this mean that any and all reports are acceptable and can be called A3-style documents? Most certainly not. As we have tried to show through the use of examples and explanation, there are standard yet flexible ways to write A3 reports for a variety of situations. Chapters 3, 4, and 5 provide some initial templates to start your thinking and personal experimentation, and are intended to minimize the frustration of merely spinning your wheels. We suggest that companies use these basic forms as "standards" or initial starting points for learning purposes but that users view them as rough guidelines that report authors will adapt to suit specific circumstances, keeping with the basic principles of A3 thinking.

A final word of caution: When adherence to a corporate template becomes paramount in usage of A3 reports, the final result is always frustration, and the process and the tool become ineffective. Efforts to standardize and maintain control are almost always well intended. However, when the overriding concern becomes control over adherence to a method rather than improvement, the creative spirit of kaizen is often lost. Form wins over substance. An old Japanese proverb translates roughly as "A fool knows just one way of doing things." The implied meaning is that an expert always knows several different ways of accomplishing the task along with the pros and cons of each way. Consider A3 report writing in the same spirit by using the tool and the templates we have provided as starting points for organizing storylines. The key point in the end is improvement and learning. Adherence to the PDCA cycle and the basic elements that we have outlined in preceding chapters has proved to be an effective, long-term approach to improving organizational performance.

Where to Start

In observing eager participants learning to use A3 reports, very often, the initial scope of the improvement effort or process analyzed is too large. This probably reflects a human tendency to underestimate difficulty or the inability to truly see the details of an operation. Many learn this lesson painfully during initial usage of the A3 reports.

Toyota has had several decades of trial-based learning-by-doing with A3s. A pattern has emerged for learning A3s, to which most within Toyota adhere when teaching A3 report writing to someone for the first time. Learners should ideally practice A3 report writing in the course of a problem-solving activity, and the scope should be limited to an area over which the report author has control. In other words, first-timers start learning A3 report writing on a fairly small, yet significant, problem that is fully within the person's area of responsibility.

Why is this important? When the scope is too large, the learner often confronts multiple problems outside of his or her control. Issues with negotiation, persuasion, control, resources, and other argumentative topics get in the way of the discussion. The focus on learning the steps of producing an A3 report is diminished, and in some cases results do not materialize and the tool is not valued as appropriate for these situations.

In reality, A3 reports can be excellent tools for persuading people in a factual, rational manner. The tool, when properly used, puts the focus on describing the process in detail and discussing in an unemotional manner what is wrong or what can be improved and how. It turns the discussion away from the five whos to the more beneficial 5 Why's. But it takes time and practice to acquire skill in using these techniques. Thus, to learn A3 thinking in a more incremental fashion, we suggest that the first foray into writing an A3 be simple and focused on a basic problem within one's realm of control that is relatively free of interference. This will allow the learner to focus on the A3 process without the complexity of interdepartmental politics and other issues. As confidence and skill in the A3 process increase, broader and more complex issues can be addressed using the tool with greater likelihood of success.

The second issue with scope control is that the broader the topic, the longer it usually takes to resolve the issue. Data collection, interviews, and analysis of many different operations are sometimes required. This is, of course, the real world in which we live and work. And A3 reports function effectively in this arena as well, because they can be used to frame broad issues just as well as deeper technical issues. The reality is that cross-functional issues often require more time and persuasion to convince people and to get the ball rolling. This length of time can be a significant learning barrier.

For the purpose of initial learning, our experience suggests that a topic that can be completed in two to four weeks is about ideal for a first project. The problem does not have to be large or excessively complex. The key point is to complete the PDCA cycle and to demonstrate the steps of A3 report writing. Learning and feedback can thus happen quickly while it is still relevant and fresh in the learner's mind. If the A3 scope is too large, the initial learning and timing of feedback occurs too slowly and key learning points and coaching opportunities are lost. Like golf or any skills-related endeavor, we suggest attempting shorter and more frequent practice sessions on the driving range in the beginning. Then, later on, you can attempt more difficult courses to test your game, so to speak.

Handwritten versus Computer-Generated A3s

Another common question we continually confront is whether to write the A3s by hand or by personal computer (PC). Having learned to write them by hand first, we are strongly in favor of this option in the beginning for several reasons. We will outline the pros and cons of each method and explain our overall position.

When Toyota and other companies started writing A3 reports in the 1960s, the issue of handwritten versus PC-generated reports was never even a question. Mainframe computers existed at that time, but neither desktop PCs nor laptop computers had yet appeared. Desktops came into use during the mid- to late-1980s at Toyota, and employee laptops were the norm by the mid-1990s. Thus, historically, the norm in the early days of A3 reports was to create the reports by hand. In hindsight, this event may have been an advantage in many respects.

A key section of the A3 is the depiction of the current condition, the second or third major step in drafting most A3 reports. When using a computer to draft the report, the immediate tendency is to type out several bulleted points. For example:

■ Long lead time
■ Buildup of too much inventory between processes
■ Push style of information flow
■ Multiple schedule points in the process

While such a description of the current state of production in this manufacturing example is not inaccurate, the words are fairly high level and general in nature. Words do not depict an image very effectively and, often, different people in the same audience will conjure up different mental images of what is being described. Furthermore, the best countermeasure is often driven by the details of a given situation, so high-level descriptions are not very useful for actual problem solving.

One way of combating this tendency is to insist on some type of picture or visual image. Drafting an image of the process has several benefits. Usually it forces the author to draw out the process in more detail than just words. It typically requires making several firsthand examinations rather than just relying upon memory. And it engages different parts of the brain in thinking about the process. When drawing out the current condition in vivid detail, suddenly more questions and thoughts arise and insights into problems also occur to the author. It is a good technique for stimulating thinking as well as for sharing information quickly and effectively.

To illustrate, consider the current state image depicted in figure 7.1 for the same problem. The image conveys much greater richness of information, including the different entities involved, how they relate, and what the important parameters are for this problem. Moreover, it is easier to see that the lead time for production is twenty-three days, and the critically important question of "why" begins to surface in the mind. The answer is not here in this picture, of course; the facts are at the production site and will require several trips to count inventory, check changeover times, and look at scheduling methods to determine in more quantitative detail why the lead time is twenty-three days. For example, a next step might be to break down the twenty-three days in some sort of Pareto chart to determine where the majority of time is spent by station, and then an even more detailed breakdown for the stations with highest delay times. The point is that all this further investigation is triggered by the image and the curiosity to find out "why" in more detail. Often words alone—such as, "the lead time is too long"—do not have this same effect.

So what is wrong with generating the image using a computer program? There are many benefits to using computers to generate A3 reports; in fact, computers are widely used today within Toyota to generate A3s (or, increasingly, A4 reports, which are half the size of an A3). The advantages are clear to most: easier editing, clearer print, faster storage and retrieval, easier dissemination (especially

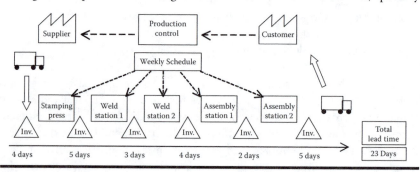

Figure 7.1   Current state of Acme Manufacturing

to geographically dispersed teams), ability to incorporate digital images, and so forth. The problem we have discovered is that when novices first learn to write A3s on a computer, the natural choice is to use a word processor style of software. The capability of drawing pictures in these types of programs is improving, but they are still quite limited and clumsy, particularly for more complex shapes and curves. The problem-solver then spends more mental effort trying to figure out how to make the software draw the image he or she wants than on understanding what is really important in the problem. To address this problem, one might try using software specifically designed for creating images, but then we face the issue of actually creating a report around the image—so the same problem persists: focusing on how to get the machine to do what you want rather than focusing on the workplace problem. These same issues carry through to other sections of the report.

The other advantage of hand-drawn A3s is that they can be quickly generated on site. This allows for rapid data capture of observations, information from interviews, and so on. It also enables very rapid feedback: "Here, I just drew a picture of how I understand this process works. Is this consistent with your understanding?" In contexts like manufacturing shops and hospital floors, where computer access may be limited or where participants physically move nonstop, a simple tool that can be drawn by hand may actually have greater receptivity. Research on boundary objects, in fact, has found that hand-drawn communication aids tend to generate more and richer discussion than computer-generated ones simply because the former is viewed as less permanent.[1]

For these reasons, we strongly recommend creating A3s by hand initially, especially when it comes to depicting the current condition. In our experience, failure to do so nearly always results in the same general pattern: The author opts for the path of least effort and types in bulleted points that are largely subjective and qualitative in nature. This shortchanges the value of the current condition section of the report and often inhibits the learner's ability to see the real problem in the process and infer any of the root causes. It also inhibits the ability of the A3 report writer to communicate the current condition with any audience that is unfamiliar with the process. This same rationale extends to the rest of the report. For these reasons, we believe taking the time to hand-draw your first few A3 reports will yield big dividends. Later on, the reports can be turned into electronic format, if necessary.

If electronic versions of A3s are a must in your organization, we still recommend initially sketching the A3 by hand before going to computer. The example A3s contained in this book are all electronically formatted, yet each was first sketched out by hand before becoming formalized into electronic format. In some ways, this approach encapsulates the best of both words. The most critical thinking in terms of problem understanding, audience needs, report structure, and overall message, and even obtaining rapid feedback can be thought through without the encumbrances of technology. Yet the electronic version of the near final version takes advantage of the benefits of technology.

Coaching

Part of the power of the A3 tool is that it makes the thinking processes of the problem-solver more visible, which enables better coaching and mentorship. Analogous to most sports, some coaching and guidance on writing an effective A3 can make a big difference. Almost all the actual training in Toyota is provided on the job, not in a classroom environment. This works well when there is a wealth of experienced talent available, as in Toyota's case. But what about companies or individuals that are trying to get started? We have three suggestions for moving forward.

The first suggestion is to use this book as a guide. There is more detail on A3 report writing in this book than exists in Toyota Motor Corporation's own training documents (in part because Toyota has no need for it since so much learning occurs on the job during the course of work). This book is our attempt to codify some of the thinking patterns, best practices, and lessons learned so that interested parties outside of Toyota can learn about the tool and process. It is not possible for us to anticipate every question or need, but it is our best shot at a starting point. In reality, there could be a book in A3 problem solving in specific contexts such as engineering or product development or hospitals to answer the many detailed questions. However, this book attempts to highlight the key points in writing A3s at a broad level, yet with enough depth so that any reader can begin experimenting with the tool on his or her own, regardless of the work environment.

A second suggestion is to seek feedback on your A3 from people you respect and trust within your organization, even if they are not experienced with A3 reports. For example, if you are blessed with a natural mentor and coaching figure at work, openly share a draft with him or her, seeking advice and input. The quality of the feedback may vary, but anyone with good problem-solving and managerial skills can probably provide some good advice and perspective on the matter in most cases. They can also help you ascertain whether and how the problem is consistent with the organization's priorities.

Simply asking many different individuals to comment on your A3-in-progress can be very useful. Internal subject matter experts can reveal useful insights on the process in question. Feedback from multiple parties on the current condition section helps ensure you have covered the process in sufficient breadth and detail. Getting input from multiple sources can balance out the learning points obtained from any one individual. While not ideal, this approach still allows you to get practical feedback from multiple sources. In the end, though, you will have to decide which points of feedback are the most relevant for your A3 report.

Seeking the counsel of good problem-solvers in your organization can also be extremely insightful, even if they do not have expertise in the issue under investigation. Since A3 thinking is a derivative of the scientific method and PDCA style of problem solving, a skilled problem-solver should be able to provide some valuable feedback on whether or not the thinking is sound and conclusions are logical. Ideally, you will find this mentoring coach, process expert, and problem-solver all in one person; but when that is not possible, seek out multiple parties.

As a final possibility, you might also want to investigate obtaining the help or advice of a consultant familiar with A3 report writing. Due to the expansion of Toyota in North America and Europe, there are increasing numbers of former employees who have entered the consulting profession. Many are no doubt very good at the basics of writing A3 reports and can help you get started on your own learning journey. However, not every person who worked for Toyota is necessarily skilled in A3 reports, just as not everyone who ever worked for GE is an expert in Six Sigma, for example. If you decide to seek external coaching support, ask to see some completed examples of A3s and obtain a sense of how he or she would teach the topic in your company. If there is a good fit, it may be a good option. If not, taking maximum advantage of internal resources is probably the better route.

Approval

Related to feedback and coaching is the approval process for A3 reports. In initial A3 writing efforts, this topic is not a major concern. However, as use of the documents gains widespread acceptance, approval will increasingly matter. To illustrate the importance of having an approval process, we will share one of the authors' experiences while in Japan.

When a new engine plant was launched in one of Toyota's facilities in North America, several automated machining lines were installed for producing engine components. In one particular case, the part-loading system for the crankshaft machining center involved a new overhead gantry style design. Several months into regular production, it began to experience malfunctions every two to three months, on average. This continued for a period of time until eventually it became a big enough problem to be placed in the top five machine downtime problems for the factory. The root cause was correctly identified to be an incorrect specification of the bearing used in the gantry device. Engineering calculations indicated that under the existing load, the bearing would fail about every three months, and with regularity that was indeed the case. The possible improvement actions included the following:

- Installing larger bearings of the same type, which would require a fairly significant redesign of portions of the gantry device
- Replacing the bearings every three months or so on a preventive maintenance schedule, which would require nearly twenty hours of work on weekends each time
- Changing from simple greased bearings to continually lubricated bearings and establishing a centralized lubrication system at a cost of $120,000

Cases such as this illustrate a clear need for an approval process. A case can be made for or against each of the solutions depending upon the needs of the moment, budget levels, timing, and the contractual liability of the original equipment manufacturer. If the person writing the A3 is allowed to make the decision alone, it might be made with too narrow a perspective and not in the best interests of the entire company.

At Toyota, approval for action items on most A3s is required by obtaining signatures from two levels above the person authoring the report, at a minimum. The logic is partially that this keeps senior personnel versed in the ongoing work of subordinates in the department. Secondly, and perhaps more importantly, more senior people generally have a greater breadth of experience, possibly having even seen the same sort of situation before, and can provide specific advice on how to proceed. The third reason is simply that often approval affects budgets, and decisions always need to be made within a context of proper fiscal stewardship. Senior personnel are usually in a better position to comment on such matters than the person writing the A3 report, or can at least require economic justifications in the A3 report.

Thus, some sort of approval system is necessary for the A3 report tool to evolve successfully into a system. Toyota's convention may not be appropriate for every organization, but some sort of convention should be established as A3 reports gain broader acceptance in practice. Here are a few ideas:

- Require signatures of different people in positions of authority for different stages of completion. For example, the background and current condition can be checked by the immediate supervisor. However, a completed A3 must be approved by the author's supervisor's boss before it is archived or widely disseminated.
- Establish budgetary guidelines for improvement projects. For example, department heads may authorize expenditures up to $5,000 while general managers can perhaps authorize amounts up to $50,000. Large amounts usually require more sign-offs. In a similar fashion, the A3 approval could go to higher levels of management depending upon cost.

■ Determine the approval authority based on the scope of the A3. Strictly intradepartmental projects need only the department head's signature, and interdepartmental issues require signatures of the heads of the departments primarily involved, and their boss(es).

The majority of A3s, however, can be written, solved, and implemented at the work-team level of the organization. Most involve more creativity than capital, from our experience. Toyota had an interesting practice of stamping a personal seal (called a *hanko* in Japanese) on the document when it was approved. By glancing at the upper right-hand corner, you could always tell who had approved the A3 so far in the company. The stamps of approval supplied credibility in many instances, or pointed out that the A3 was still in the discussion stages in other cases. Either point was often worth knowing when reading an A3.

One company we are working with is in the process of establishing a management-by-proposal ethic among its management ranks. Rather than supervisors telling subordinates what to do when facing a problem, they ask the subordinates to propose a solution to the problem in the form of an A3 report. This simultaneously engages the creative powers of each individual in the group, while creating wonderfully rich opportunities to mentor.

Storage and Retrieval

A final question that frequently arises is, "What do I do with the report once it is completed and approved? It would be nice if it could be made available for future reference." We agree that it would be nice, especially since A3s capture a good deal of thinking and learning; but the storage and retrieval question is not, in our estimation, a showstopper on tool adoption.

Toyota uses a highly decentralized and fairly informal method for storage of A3 reports. Each person keeps his or her own A3 reports in a desk drawer or on individual laptops. Copies are made or e-mailed on an as-needed basis. Knowledge of who has written a report on a given topic is not centralized but is held in the general organizational network of contacts. Another reason Toyota requires approval at two levels higher than the A3 author's position is to increase the breadth and visibility of who has done what. If the A3 contains some sort of breakthrough learning, it is nominated for inclusion in the company's quarterly engineering journal, the *Toyota Technical Review*. Other detailed technical advancements are also compiled into up-to-date standards, such as the Toyota Manufacturing Regulations and Toyota Manufacturing Standards, as needed. Most A3 reports, however, still reside mainly in desk drawers and on individual computer hard drives.

As larger numbers of A3 reports are generated, it may be powerful to have a more centralized way to store, search, and retrieve them so that knowledge generated and captured can be accessed and reused in future problem solving. One easy way to do this with electronic A3s is enabled by modern search technologies. Completed and approved A3 reports can simply be saved to a file share, which can then be searched using a software tool such as Google Desktop by anyone with access to the share. It is not too big of a stretch of imagination to envision a centralized database for storing A3s, or even specialized software applications for the creation, approval, storage, and retrieval of A3 reports. While such infrastructure may be useful, the first step is to build within the organization a strong capacity to create meaningful and useful documents. Only once this capability has been established do we recommend giving much thought to sophisticated storage and retrieval systems.

Summary

This chapter has covered several basic points regarding support structures for a system of organizational improvement based on A3 report writing. A number of them are critical for ensuring the success of writing high-quality, useful A3 reports. In particular we emphasize the following:

- Do not become slave to a format, but use the format as a standard for starting your A3 reports.
- Pay close attention to scope control, especially when first starting out. Start on something relatively easy and within your realm of control for the first attempt.
- Rely upon handwritten images, especially at first, for the current condition and other sections of the A3 where images or charts work better than pictures. Once your skill has improved or the content finalized, migrate over to electronic formats. Above all, avoid the pitfall of just listing bulleted points, a practice that is 100 percent unacceptable within Toyota because it does not advance the thinking process.
- Find a good mentor or problem-solving coach (or perhaps a small network of coaches) who can provide useful feedback on your A3s.
- Set some practical guidelines in place for approving A3 reports. This may be accomplished by designating certain levels of the organization for approval or tying the report to a budget type of approval process when cost is involved.
- Simple, decentralized methods for storing and retrieving A3 reports in the company are, at least initially, sufficient to begin the A3 journey.

Endnotes

1 K. Henderson, "Flexible Sketches and Inflexible Databases: Visual Communication, Conscription Devices, and Boundary Objects in Design Engineering." Science, Technology, and Human Values, vol. 16, no. 4 (1991): 448–73.

Chapter 8

Conclusion

Throughout this book, we introduced the basic tenants of A3 thinking. Now that you have a basic understanding of the material, we hope that you will take some time to practice this valuable skill set. Like many things in life, mastery of this topic is not gained in a single session or a short time frame. Skill in A3 report writing increases over time with practice and effort. Most people in managerial positions at Toyota have spent a couple of decades writing in this style and are still honing their skills every day.

We had several purposes in mind in writing this book on A3 thinking. For starters, it was intended as an introductory guide on A3 basics to a general audience of professionals interested in becoming practitioners of the material. In every industry or economic sector, managers and other professionals must address problems and propose changes in order to improve. In fact, Toyota uses A3 reports in every aspect of its business, from production and engineering to purchasing, sales, and finance. So we have attempted to provide general descriptions that can be readily transferred to many sectors. Second, this book was intended as an initial training vehicle, including examples, illustrations, and short exercises as a way to get started learning. Practice the material as suggested, and you should be on your way to improving your skills in this subject. Third, we hope this book will function also as a reference manual as you progress on your learning journey. From time to time, as you work on drafting A3s, we hope you will return to this material and review the highlights of each chapter.

We will now review the key points highlighted in the preceding chapters and attempt to synthesize them into what is hopefully by now a familiar framework. We conclude with some specific points of advice. Rereading this conclusion from time to time should help you recall the main points of the book without having to review every chapter. For more details, you can always consult the specific chapter in question as needed.

PDCA and Managerial Effectiveness

The Toyota Production System (TPS) has been flourishing for over fifty years and has become a fixture in the popular media for almost two decades now. Countless articles and attempts to explain the system have been undertaken during the past several decades. Different books have been written about the tools and the system in great detail, and they are quite good. Interestingly, the top-selling books in Japan on TPS are written by Western authors such as Jeffrey Liker, Daniel Jones, and James Womack. A somewhat self-critical assessment of the situation, however, is that although we in the West have become fairly proficient in talking about or describing the system, we are unfortunately still not all that adept at implementing it on our own.

In fairness, most companies today are still in the infancy of their lean journey. Rigorous TPS implementation in Toyota began around 1950. But the TPS of the mid-1950s was not much more than a few efficient machine shops under the management of Taiichi Ohno and Eiji Toyoda. It took years for TPS to spread and take hold across the company. The early pilot areas were simply called the Ohno Lines and indeed were just that: pilots and experiments in learning about how to apply TPS.

Interestingly, Toyota did not bother to document or start calling its system TPS until around 1973. Until that time, Toyota was content to solve problems and constantly improve quality, lower costs, increase productivity, and improve other key metrics while developing human resources. There was no need to officially call it anything since everyone internally understood it was just the Toyota way of doing things. In 1973, however, the Toyota Education and Training Department drafted the first internal manual describing TPS. The preface was authored by former vice president of manufacturing Taiichi Ohno, and the former president and chairman Fujio Cho was a major contributor. The editor of the document was Isao Kato, who was kind enough to offer some advice on *Understanding A3 Thinking*.

On page 3 of the first TPS manual, the authors offer an important piece of advice. "TPS is founded upon a scientific mindset. On the shop floor are various problems. It is important to start with those phenomena and search for the true root cause by tracing things to their origin. In other words, we place heavy importance upon getting the facts."[1]

The background of this thinking, according to Isao Kato, comes from multiple sources. The first was simply the culture of the company tracing back to its founders, Sakichi Toyoda and his son, Kiichiro Toyoda. Both gentlemen were noted engineers and inventors in Japan and established the early culture of Toyota and its inventive spirit. The second input was the sheer personality of Taiichi Ohno and his insistence upon going to the shop floor or *genba* in order to observe things firsthand and identify the root cause of a problem. "Practice over Theory" was the title he gave to his foreword in the 1973 TPS manual. In words as well as in action, Ohno molded the culture of the shop floor and management by force of sheer personality and willpower. The third input was the exposure to American management concepts prevalent in the 1950s and 1960s, such as the Training within Industry (TWI) material as well as the basic philosophy of Plan-Do-Check-Act (PDCA).

The collective influence of these sources, and no doubt others, helped establish the early mind-set of the company. Problems were opportunities to be solved or improved and not to be ignored. Tools familiar to lean practitioners today, such as kanban, value stream mapping, or standardized work, were not taught and trained early on. Those items were derived and developed as countermeasures or analysis techniques in the course of problem-solving specific issues.

The development of one lean manufacturing tool, the single-minute exchange of stamping dies (SMED) technique, is an interesting case in point.[2] One of the authors had the opportunity to interview Mr. Katsuya Jibiki, a former head of the stamping shops in Toyota. When asked how SMED was developed and implemented in the 1960s, he shook his head and said, "It really didn't happen that way."[3] Instead of inventing or implementing a SMED program, he related the background of how they were trying to improve operational availability on press machines and solve the problem of parts not being available in the welding shops and, in turn, to the final assembly areas on time.

The current situation or symptom at that time was making the wrong parts at the wrong time and in too large a batch size. Batch sizes were large because the stamping die changeover time was long. Analysis showed multiple reasons for the lengthy changeover process such as poor preparation, excessive motion, rough die alignment methods, and many other small problems. What then ensued was several years of repeated problem-solving work, machine by machine, implementing specific action items in response to specific problems contributing to long changeover times. Ultimately, the department achieved an average changeover time of fifteen minutes by 1962, down from several hours.[4] Smaller stamping machines were all in the single-minute range by then. Stamping engineers spread what worked to other areas and eventually to new machines. In doing so, specific methods were codified for reducing changeover time, much of which is known today as SMED. In other words, the process was one closely aligned with what we have called A3 thinking in this text, and one very consistent with the scientific method and PDCA-style problem solving.

A3 Thinking

Just calling A3 thinking "problem solving" does not do justice to the topic or the efforts put forth by Toyota in developing its human resources over the past several decades. If mere problem solving and training were the issue, the world outside of Toyota would have been able to copy its production system by now. The production system of Toyota, of course, includes specific beliefs and actions regarding how to schedule production and produce to a takt time, how to standardize work practices, how to build in quality, and how to maintain machines, for example. Those topic-specific practices have been the scope of many other works and are not our focus here. Instead, we have endeavored to show the common paradigm or thinking pattern behind the development and practical implementation of those tools and techniques.

Specifically, as noted in chapter 2, the overall style of thinking within Toyota surrounding A3s can be characterized by a handful of interrelated elements. The first telling feature is that of a logical thinking process. Neither A3 thinking nor the Toyota Production System is mysterious when explained by the person responsible for his or her respective area in question. It is an eminently logical method to address the situation in one's realm of control. The presenter in Toyota usually goes to great lengths to explain that while this is not ideal, it is the best state possible under the current methods.

The second salient feature of A3 thinking is that of objectivity. Employees in Toyota are coached to be detailed, quantitative, and specific in their characterizations of the current state or any form of problem solving. The reason is that subjective opinions have no business in science, engineering, or the basic process of kaizen. The main cause of many arguments and time-wasting meetings is due to the inability of the personnel in the organization to speak in objective terms. As a result, exchanges of opinion become heated and positions become entrenched. In Toyota, primary emphasis is placed upon getting to the root cause of an issue by asking the five whys as needed. The emphasis is placed upon coaching learners to see the process clearly and not merely fall into the trap of assigning blame to some group or individual.

Additionally, Toyota management strongly emphasizes results and process. In recent times, this has become known as the Toyota way. Performance pressure applied to all aspects of the business is needed to achieve world-class results. Any company that aspires to have the highest volume, the highest profits, and the highest quality in its industry must have this sort of drive. However, the results cannot come at the expense of people or the process, for doing so would make the results short-lived. Deeply embedded in the psyche of the company is the notion of respect for people and doing things in a certain way. The way, of course, depends upon the circumstances and changes over time. Yet the emphasis on both results and process helps maintain a healthy balance in the company.

The other aspects we mentioned in describing A3 thinking were those of synthesis, alignment, coherency, and a systems viewpoint. These features each describe an aspect of the A3 thinking pattern within the company. A3 reports are identifiable by size but also because of the way in which they are written. A well-written report is an effective synthesis that describes the situation and promotes alignment and coherency within the organization on a given topic. The topic is written in an objective manner, where facts trump either theory or parochial behavior. The content ideally depicts a systems viewpoint on what is truly best for the current situation or company and explains why in a persuasive manner. In fact, consensus on the report by all those who may be impacted is central to Toyota's implementation of A3 reports. The combination of these factors is a difficult skill to master and one of the reasons that it takes a while to become a skilled practitioner.

Three Main Types

In chapters 3, 4, and 5, we attempted to describe several basic types of A3 reports in fairly concrete terms. In reality, no two reports ever look alike as each one deals with a unique topic or process. Nonetheless, there are three broad categories of A3s that we identified in discussions with long-time practitioners within Toyota. Those three types, broadly speaking, are for problem solving, proposal writing, and status reviews.

All new employees start out in the company by practicing the problem-solving style of A3s. The contents follow a fairly standard and logical order similar to the pattern found in quality control circles and the PDCA style of problem solving. In general, the pattern is to identify the background, depict the current state in detail, set a target or goal, analyze the root causes in the process, implement action items, verify results, and then standardize in the event of positive outcomes. If the goal is not achieved, the cycle is repeated. The verbal description is quite easy. Following the pattern, getting into the details, and achieving results is always another matter. This learning cycle and pattern of action is considered critical for all employees in the company.

The other two main types of A3s are for proposal writing and reviewing the progress of either projects or proposals. Each type follows the basic PDCA style of thinking but emphasizes a different part of the cycle. The former type is most often used up front to propose and justify a new policy or course of action with the process, team, or department. The latter is to review the outcome of any sort of project or implementation work after the fact. As such, they emphasize different parts of the PDCA cycle. For starting purposes, we highly recommend working on a basic problem-solving A3 first before attempting the latter types.

Within Toyota, all types of A3 undergo review at various stages of development. Peers and mentors review the reports for accuracy, coherency, thoroughness, and overall communication effectiveness. The Toyota ethic requires report authors to synthesize as much feedback from individuals or departments potentially affected by the author's work or ideas as possible. If an individual's concerns could not be addressed, as a courtesy, the author meets with that person to explain why. Furthermore, someone with appropriate authority approves each A3. In many ways, this is a process check (has the person exhibited A3 thinking?) and represents a tremendous mentoring opportunity, because the A3 report makes the person's problem-solving approach and logic visible.

Form and Style

As a practical matter, in chapter 6, we offered some advice regarding the form and style of writing A3 reports. Much of the advice is derived from Toyota's own training materials, augmented by our own research and experience. As the name implies, the most obvious feature of an A3 is its size: roughly 11 x 17 inches or the international paper size identified as A3. The size alone, however, is not what makes an A3. Some reports within Toyota are actually three A4 pages, each roughly 8½ x 11 inches; others are one A4 page in length. The structure of the document and the format described in the three types is what makes the document an A3 report.

Within an A3, we feel some stylistic guidelines are worth striving to meet. The content is to be brief, yet detailed and well organized. Endless lists of bulleted points and wordy opinions are not acceptable. A frequent criticism of initial A3s drawn by Western parties is the tendency to utilize straight narrative or bulleted lists. The result is an A3 that is qualitative in nature and lacks the visual appearance of a more advanced one.

Rather than words, the best advice we can provide is to urge practitioners to draw pictures or diagrams wherever possible to convey their ideas, observations, and findings. The Japanese probably have an inherent advantage in this aspect, because their writing system is based upon pictorial characters. However, with some creativity, almost anyone can use flow diagrams, sketches, tables, graphs, and other illustrative forms to generate a clear picture of events.

Final Advice

An anecdote often heard in describing Toyota is the tale from India of four blind men stumbling upon an elephant in a clearing. Upon discovering the animal, the blind men each latch onto a part of the animal and begin to describe it. One hugs the leg and says it is round like a tree trunk. Another holds the tail and says the elephant is like a rope. A third has the trunk and says it is some sort of hose and attached to something larger. Another pushes against the side and says it is rough and sturdy like a wall.

All of the blind men are "correct," but they are all also "wrong" with their conclusion. The discovery of TPS and identification of the system is much like this analogy. It has been described by learners as QC circles, kanban, JIT, standardized work, kaizen workshops, value stream mapping, and many other methods and techniques. These are all accurate at some level and can work to drive improvement in some fashion. However, in the end, they are just tools for improvement.

From our experience, improvement efforts in companies become ineffective when the emphasis becomes adhering to a standard tool and enforcing a certain way of doing things. Inherently, the adherence is all well intended as a means of promoting standardization and ultimately improvement. Unfortunately, the implementation of a certain tool or technique can become more important than improvement of the process or current situation. In other words, the means trump the ends. Thus our concluding piece of advice to avoid the trap of suddenly mandating A3 report writing or making it the latest fad method for implementing your version of lean manufacturing. In other words, place the emphasis on performing, improving, and learning rather than on conforming to templates, tools, or procedures.

The amazing thing about the Toyota Production System is that it has continued to make sense for over fifty years of continued operation and to deliver operational and financial results. The tools and techniques have changed over the years as a kanban in 1950 looks different from a kanban in 1980, and who knows what it will look like in 2020? The key point within Toyota is that employees have all been taught a general, rigorous pattern of thinking for improvement of all aspects of the business. In reflecting upon the importance and success of the system, we strongly believe it is these thinking patterns and skills that are the key to the company's long-term success, and not just the mere tools. We hope this book is a first step in helping to decipher one of those thinking patterns more clearly. Good luck with your own A3 thinking!

Endnotes

1 F. Cho, T. Ohno, K. Sugimori, et al., *Toyota Production System—Toyota Methods*, edited by I. Kato, internal publication by the Education and Training Department, Toyota Motor Corporation (January 1973).

2 We hope the reader not familiar with manufacturing will allow us to indulge in this example, as it concretely illustrates the importance of problem solving over tool implementation. For those unfamiliar, stamping is a manufacturing technology for forming parts out of sheet metal by slamming together two hardened pieces of steel ("dies") that have been carefully machined into forms that will produce parts of the desired shape. The machines that slam the dies together are called presses. Presses can make any kind of sheet metal part by changing out the die set. In stamping automobile parts, this is a significant task because the dies can weigh several thousand pounds, traditionally taking several hours from the last part stamped on the old die set to the first good part stamped on the new. Decreasing the die changeover time enables the company to more quickly switch to producing a different part and thus respond more quickly to changes.

3 Interview notes with Katsuya Jibiki, former assistant general manager of stamping, Toyota Motor Corporation, by Art Smalley, July 2006.

4 M. Cusumano, *The Japanese Automobile Industry: Technology and Management at Nissan and Toyota* (Cambridge, MA: Council on East Asian Studies and Harvard University Press, 1985), 284–85.

About the Authors

Durward K. Sobek II is an associate professor of industrial and management engineering at Montana State University. He is a recognized expert in product development systems, and has been researching and observing Toyota for many years. He has recently researched application of the A3 methodology to health care and product development, and has authored numerous articles, given presentations, and conducted workshops on this award-winning work.

Art Smalley is president of Art of Lean, a consulting company specializing in advanced TPS implementation. Art was hired and trained as a manufacturing engineer with Toyota in Japan to support the startup of Toyota facilities overseas. During his tenure with the company, he was immersed in the culture of Toyota and A3 report-writing methods by his Toyota mentors. Art authored the Shingo Research Prize award-winning workbook *Creating Level Pull* in conjunction with the Lean Enterprise Institute in 2003. More recently, in the spring of 2006, Art was inducted into the Shingo Manufacturing Prize Academy for lifetime contributions in the field of lean manufacturing.

Appendix A

"Reducing Bill Drop Time" Problem-Solving A3 Report

In this appendix, we provide a sample of a problem-solving A3 report as a possible "solution" to the exercise found near the conclusion of chapter 3. We trust that you have created at least a first draft of an A3 report based on the information provided. You can now compare the one you wrote with the example provided. Please remember that there are myriad ways the report can be written, and although some may be more effective than others, there is no one right answer! Please use this as a learning exercise to deepen your understanding of A3 thinking and to pick up some tips on the skill of A3 report writing.

You will find the complete sample problem-solving A3 report at the end of this appendix (figure A.8). In the pages that immediately follow, we walk you through the report, section by section, and offer brief explanations to help you better understand how we approached each section—and why. For each section, we comment on three aspects: 1) the strengths of this approach, 2) probable comments this approach will draw during a review, and 3) possible suggestions to consider. These are not the only aspects to consider regarding the document; however, they are some things worth mentioning or reinforcing for learning purposes. Also, the report author will not likely be able to address all of the questions in the report but will want to have thought about them and be ready to discuss the issues thoughtfully with reviewers.

To maximize the learning benefit from the exercise, we suggest the following sequence:

1. Read chapter 3 in this book.
2. Attempt part 1 of the exercise found near the end of chapter 3 (that is, draft your own A3).
3. Compare your A3 to the one found at the end of this appendix.
4. Attempt part 2 of the exercise found near the end of chapter 3. Critique one of the A3s (yours or the one provided) using the generic review questions found in table 3.1.
5. Finally, read the rest of this appendix and compare our critique to yours.

Background

Strengths of the Section

The background section (figure A.1) is quite clear, concise, and to the point. The reader can easily navigate this section quickly to obtain the gist of the report. Note also that the author assumes audience familiarity with terms such as "A/R Days" and "bill drop," so he or she does not take the space to define them.

Probable Review Questions or Comments

Reviewers will probably want to ask the following types of questions, and the author should anticipate and prepare for them in advance as much as possible. Is this a large priority for the hospital? How does this project relate to the organization's goals? Because "accounts receivable days" is mentioned, how much has it increased (or how does it compare to some benchmark)? Is there any way these comments can be quantified?

Suggestions to Consider

Make the extent of the change in accounts receivable days clear. Quantify the effects of the items mentioned and consider putting them into a trend chart, if possible.

> • ER charts frequently wait for transcriptions, resulting in delayed bill drop.
>
> • Delayed bill drop directly increases A/R days.
>
> • HIM staff experience many work arounds, delays related to ER charts

Figure A.1

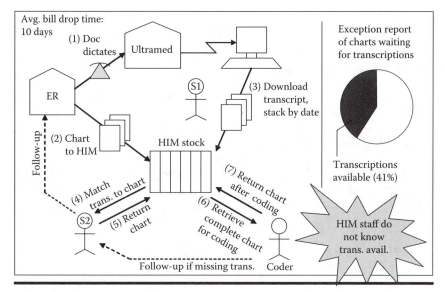

Figure A.2

Current Condition

Strengths of the Section

The obvious characteristic of the current condition section shown in figure A.2 is the visual image that depicts the work flow. The image helps the reader see the nature of the work and the basic situation in the area. This is vastly superior to attempting to explain the work flow by words alone. Use of icons also adds richness to the visual and is superior to using a standard flow chart. Further, the author has quantified the extent of the issue by use of the pie chart.

Probable Review Questions or Comments

Does the actual work flow follow the process as depicted? Are there any steps omitted here that may be useful to know? What is the actual problem in the current state? How long has this been a problem and to what extent is it increasing or decreasing? What is the sample size of the pie chart and is this data representative?

Suggestions to Consider

If possible, make the flow easier for the reader to follow. Consider if there is a way to depict the actual condition yet still make it simple for the reader to see the sequence of work. At a minimum, enlarge the sequential numbers provided or make them more noticeable somehow. It is also always advisable to identify the number of the items in the pie chart for clarity (for example, is this a sample size of one day or 1,000 observations?). Make the problem statement clearer and quantify it for a more rigorous problem statement.

Goal Statement

Strengths of the Section

The goal statement in figure A.3 provides the reader with a quantitative target that is at once both easy to see and easy to read. This goal is in line with the information presented in the background and current condition sections.

Probable Review Questions or Comments

What has bill drop time averaged historically in past years? More or less than the ten days referenced? In other words, is this condition normal in historic terms or has something made it worse recently? Is it sufficient to measure and track only one metric for progress? Or are there any other metrics that should be measured as well, such as the variability or range of bill drop times or accounts receivable? Is this 30 percent improvement goal aggressive enough? What is the target completion date for this goal?

Suggestions to Consider

Goal statements should always reflect a few simple principles. They should be specific and measurable, and they should show the expected target date for goal attainment. In this case, the author might consider altering the goal statement so that it reads something like, "Decrease the bill drop rate 30%, from 10 days to 7 days" for clarity. The author may also want to indicate when the target will be reached (such as the end of the month or quarter) in order to be more specific and less open-ended. Another factor to consider is whether any other metrics such as productivity, quality, or other areas (such as accounts receivable days) should be tracked as well. Often, it is easy to improve one metric while unintentionally sacrificing another.

• Bill drop rate < 7.0 days.

Figure A.3

HIM coders do not know transcriptions are sitting in HIM.
↳ Staff member S2 did not attach transcription.
  ↳ Staff member S2 did not find transcription in stack or misidentified.
    ↳ Staff member S1 missed transcriptions, or misfiled in the stack.
      ↳ No clear, consistent signal from ER that dictations have been done.

Figure A.4

Cause Analysis

Strengths of the Section

The root cause analysis summary displayed in figure A.4 effectively uses the popular 5 Why's technique for ascertaining the root cause of the problem. Each step answers a "why?" question of the previous one. This is an excellent method to apply when you have only one main cause to investigate in order to solve the problem.

Probable Review Questions or Comments

Is there really only one cause for this problem? Are there other aspects of the 4Ms (manpower, machine, material, method) or environment that should also be considered, for example? Other than deduction, is there any way to test this notion of the root cause? If not, is there a further step on the 5 Why's tree regarding why there is no clear signal from the ER that dictations have been done? Or can the analysis truly stop at this level in order to produce a countermeasure? In other words, is this really the root cause?

Suggestions to Consider

It might be worthwhile to show an Ishikawa (or fishbone) diagram in addition to the 5 Why's diagram, especially if there is more than one root cause to consider. The fishbone can show multiple causes where the 5 Why's leads only to one. The right analysis depends on the situation. Other more quantitative techniques can be used as well in more complex instances. In any case, consider how best to establish cause and effect, and then communicate it to the reader. Can the hypothesized cause and intended effect either be made more quantitative or estimated?

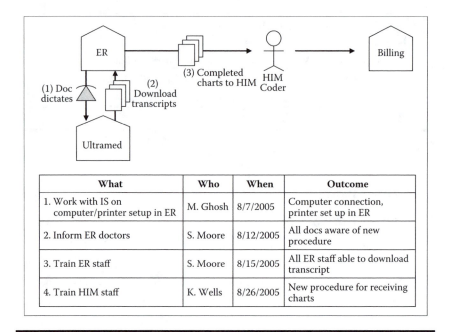

What	Who	When	Outcome
1. Work with IS on computer/printer setup in ER	M. Ghosh	8/7/2005	Computer connection, printer set up in ER
2. Inform ER doctors	S. Moore	8/12/2005	All docs aware of new procedure
3. Train ER staff	S. Moore	8/15/2005	All ER staff able to download transcript
4. Train HIM staff	K. Wells	8/26/2005	New procedure for receiving charts

Figure A.5

Countermeasures

Strengths of the Section

The counter measures section (figure A.5) does a nice job of showing the intended flow of work with the proposed changes in place. It also highlights the main countermeasure action items with regard to who will do what by when. This method effectively shows the reader the gist of the work accomplished.

Probable Review Questions or Comments

Because there is only one main countermeasure, is it really addressing the root cause of the current problem? Might there be a deeper root cause or system improvement potential beyond shifting the transcription download responsibility from HIM to ER? Are there other alternative countermeasures not listed here that were considered or should also be considered for some reason? Will the implemented countermeasure prevent recurrence of the problem with a high degree of certainty? Can the countermeasure be tested in any simple way for confirmation?

Suggestions to Consider

It is best practice in A3 report writing to make explicit the relationship between the indicated root cause and the countermeasures. In this case, the author could simply add a cloudburst containing a phrase such as "simplified ER-HIM connection" to highlight that the main motivation behind the work flow change was to address the root cause identified. Ideally, the author would also strive to show the anticipated or demonstrated effect of the countermeasures if there is more than one countermeasure (stating which action has the biggest impact and why). Training is often an action item but normally not an acceptable root cause or countermeasure. Always consider what else can be done to prevent recurrence of the problem in the future and ideally "mistake-proof" the process.

Check

Strengths of the Section

The check statement displayed in figre A-6 shows that a measurable impact has been demonstrated versus the goal over an eleven-day period. Fewer charts are received without transcripts, and the bill drop rate has been reduced to less than seven days. This indicates that the team has made clear progress toward the goal.

Probable Review Questions or Comments

Is this period of time large enough to be considered representative and confirm progress toward the goal? What else could have occurred during this period of time that might also have affected the result? Are there any other metrics that need to be checked to make certain that some other metric has not worsened? Why did some charts still not have transcripts? Was the initial goal set stringent enough, or was it too easy an improvement goal?

Suggestions to Consider

Consider whether another metric needs to be added to provide proper balance. Make sure that neither quality nor productivity has been adversely affected while

---

Charts from 10/10/2005 –10/21/2005 checked

• 5 of 371 charts received without transcript (1.3%)

• Average bill drop rate = 6.55 days

Figure A.6

reducing bill drop time, for example. Perhaps show the improvement from 10 days to 6.55 days as a trend chart, and also show the percentage improvement. Show which action items contributed the most toward the improvement if there were multiple actions implemented. Perhaps also show whether the change has had any effect on accounts receivable days.

Follow-Up

Strengths of the Section

The final section of the A3 (figure A.7) lists several clear points to be considered for follow-up actions. The list is short and concise and is easy to read for the audience. It focuses on 1) shoring up the remaining defects, 2) making sure other parts of the organization are not adversely affected by the change, and 3) pressing for additional improvement.

Probable Review Questions or Comments

Is there any reason to shorten the bill drop time even further beyond the 6.55-day level already achieved? Why or why not? If so, by how much and what sort of effort might this entail? Who is going to do the remaining items identified in this section and by when? Is there any other part of the hospital that can duplicate these gains?

Suggestions to Consider

Consider framing the remaining actions in a table with a better indication of who will do what by when. Indicate whether any other sections of the hospital can also achieve these sorts of improvements by sharing the methods and learning points. Mention whether there are any other hospital units or affiliated hospitals with which the results should be shared. How can the hospital make sure this change becomes a permanent part of the process? If there are any implications for future purchase of technology or equipment, note that fact for additional discussion and planning purposes.

> • Determine cause of charts arriving in HIM without transcript, and remedy.
>
> • Investigate ways to further reduce bill drop rate. Coding time is < 0.5 hr per chart typical; thus further time reductions may be possible.
>
> • Verify with billing dept. that coding continues to be accurate.

Figure A.7

Summary of A3 Report Review

We hope that you were able to discern from the preceding sections that reviewing A3 reports may be as important as writing them! There is nothing "wrong" with the A3 example provided here, and there is a great deal that is "right." And yet, there are still numerous potential points for improvement. We hope that you learned a great deal from writing your own A3, reading this one, and then considering the feedback points outlined in this appendix.

Because there is no such thing as a "perfect" A3, be careful not to spend too much time attempting to fine-tune the report in ways that are not very productive. That said, however, A3s often need to be written several times in order to improve the contents to the point of acceptance. Trade-offs and decisions on what and what not to present, and how valuable the information is versus how much resource it will take to compile it, occur frequently. Over time, you will become better at making these decisions. And, of course, the best answer often depends upon the audience and specifics of the situation. The best way to learn is to just get started, and then have somebody (or several somebodies) review the A3 and give feedback.

The complete A3 report is shown on the next couple of pages for your reference.

Theme: Reducing Bill Drop Time of Emergency Patients

Background

- ER charts frequently wait for transcriptions, resulting in delayed bill drop.
- Delayed bill drop directly increases A/R days.
- HIM staff experience many work-arounds, delays related to ER charts.

Current Condition

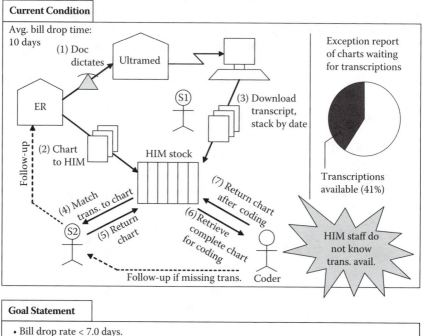

Goal Statement

- Bill drop rate < 7.0 days.

Cause Analysis

HIM coders do not know transcriptions are sitting in HIM.
↳ Staff member S2 did not attach transcription.
 ↳ Staff member S2 did not find transcription in stack or misidentified.
  ↳ Staff member S1 missed transcriptions, or misfiled in the stack.
   ↳ No clear, consistent signal from ER that dictations have been done.

Figure A.8a   Reducing Bill Drop Time of Emergency Patients A3

To: S. Moore, K. Wells

From: M. Ghosh

Date: 11/19/2005

Countermeasures

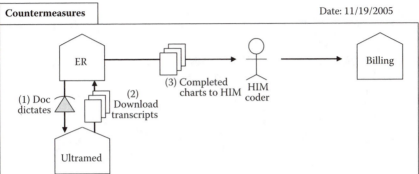

What	Who	When	Outcome
1. Work with IS on computer/printer setup in ER	M. Ghosh	8/7/2005	Computer connection, printer set up in ER
2. Inform ER doctors	S. Moore	8/12/2005	All docs aware of new procedure
3. Train ER staff	S. Moore	8/15/2005	All ER staff able to download transcript
4. Train HIM staff	K. Wells	8/26/2005	New procedure for receiving charts

Check

Charts from 10/10/2005 –10/21/2005 checked

- 5 of 371 charts received without transcript (1.3%)
- Average bill drop rate = 6.55 days

Follow-up Actions

- Determine cause of charts arriving in HIM without transcript, and remedy.
- Investigate ways to further reduce bill drop rate. Coding time is < 0.5 hr per chart typical; thus further time reductions may be possible.
- Verify with billing dept. that coding continues to be accurate.

Figure A.8b   Reducing Bill Drop Time of Emergency Patients A3

Appendix B

"Practical Problem Solving" Proposal A3 Report

In chapter 4, we introduced the standard A3 tool used for proposal writing. At the end of that chapter, we suggested an exercise to test your skill and build up capability with this type of A3. In this appendix, we provide a sample proposal A3 report for that exercise, for purposes of comparison to the one you have drafted. Because the A3 can be written in a multiplicity of ways, we offer a few words of commentary on each section to help you gain some insight into why we wrote it the way we did. Other approaches can be equally valid, given the author's personal style, core message, and audience. As in appendix A, we also provide some probable comments or questions from a hypothetical reviewer and offer some suggestions to improve the report.

You may find it helpful to first review the complete A3 report found at the end of this appendix (figure B.7) and conduct your own critique using the questions in chapter 4 (table 4.1) before reading our commentary. This will give you practice reviewing a proposal A3 and will enhance your learning from the exercise.

- Defects up 30+% over last 12 months in manufacturing
- Supervisor and lead person turnover in past 12 months is close to 50%
- Need to reduce defects to meet corporate goals set out for manufacturing operations in '07
- Opportunity to improve workforce skills and develop human resources in manufacturing

Figure B.1

Background

Strengths of the Section

The main points of this background section (figure 8.1) are fairly clear, concise, and easy for the audience to read. The reader can easily navigate this section quickly to obtain the gist of the report. The author chose to communicate the background using a bulleted list due to the assumed familiarity of the audience with the broader issues of concern.

Probable Review Questions or Comments

Reviewers will probably ask the following types of questions, which the author should anticipate and prepare for in advance as much as possible. How important is this issue for the company? How does it align to any specific goals this year? Is the turnover in supervisory personnel related to the increase in defects?

Suggestions to Consider

Clarify the scope of the work clearly to avoid any potential confusion. Consider showing a combination chart showing the trend for defects in conjunction with the change in supervisory staff. This creates a simple correlation check that may be needed.

Current Condition

Strengths of the Section

The main characteristic of the current condition section shown in figure B.2 is the use of a pie chart and Pareto chart for depicting the situation, with categorical breakdowns of data gathered on product defects. These two charts help frame and clarify the current situation with respect to defects. The author also summarizes his conclusion of the data (that is, that all manufacturing defects were preventable). He further summarizes the results of a personnel survey on

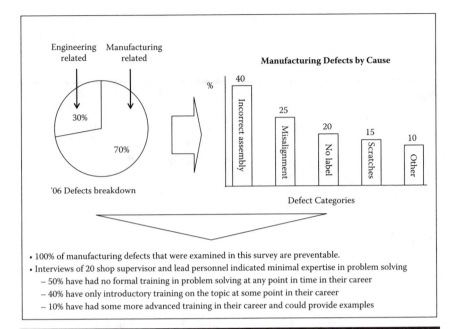

Figure B.2

problem-solving skills that presumably flowed from asking why preventable defects were not prevented.

Probable Review Questions or Comments

How many total defects were there in 2006 (that is, what is the sample size)? How does this relate to 2005 and the years before? Has anything changed in the product, process, or something else outside of the people part of the equation that could account for the increase in defects? Is the survey sample size large enough to represent the supervisor population?

Suggestions to Consider

Since this is a hypothetical proposal, we are taking for granted that the increase in supervisor turnover and the increase in defects are somehow linked. If this point is uncertain, however, the linkage or correlation should be made more clearly in this section, for example, through a combination chart with turnover and defects trend shown together. Then, as a further drill down, a comparison of the previous supervisor skill level in problem solving versus the current super-

---

• Implement a practical problem-solving training program over the next quarter in manufacturing
  – Reduce defects by over 50% by the end of the year in manufacturing
  – Improve the problem-solving capability of existing personnel

---

Figure B.3

visor problem-solving level could be depicted in a table for comparison. None-theless, even if these points are valid assumptions, the author may still want to consider turning the bulleted points about supervisor skill level into a matrix, table, or chart for ease in viewing.

Proposal

Strengths of the Section

The proposal statement in figure B.3 indicates the general intent of the proposed work for this project. The points are concise and fairly clear, and they indicate the timing of the action at a high level. The author also includes a measurable target.

Probable Review Questions or Comments

How certain is the author that this action item is necessary to achieve the target? Are there other action items as well (outside the scope of this proposal) that will need to be worked on by other parties? Why does the current group of supervisors have weaker problem-solving skills than the previous generation? Does this aspect of the situation or the increased turnover in supervisory personnel need to be looked at separately? How confident is the author that a 50 percent reduction in defects can be achieved by the end of the year by this proposal?

Suggestions to Consider

The scope and content of the proposal hinge upon the linkage between the increase in defects and the supervisor turnover. If this linkage is clear in the minds of management, the proposal is on track. If not, before this proposal goes forward, it should be satisfactorily clarified. Assuming the linkage (and hence the basis for this proposal) was accepted to be true, the proposal might still be altered by showing more clearly which defects in manufacturing would likely be reduced and to what target level by increasing the supervisor skill levels.

	Criteria		
Alternatives	*Cost*	*Quality*	*Timing*
A. Hire external resource for training and implementation	$40K	High	Mid-June
B. Utilize training at a local community college	$15K	Medium	June
C. Use internal resources and develop materials	N/A	Medium	May

<u>**Overall Comments:**</u>
- Target consultant group available and has proven experience with affiliate company in the area. However, they cannot support the training until mid-June due to resource constraints.
- Local community college course does not start until the June summer session begins and training would be off site. Follow-up support possible.
- Internal resources could be diverted on short notice. One person from training and development and one full-time resource from manufacturing would be required to support the training and roll-out.

Figure B.4

Evaluation of Alternatives

Strengths of the Section

The next section (figure B.4) outlines the three options put forth for consideration regarding the problem-solving training proposal. The matrix outlines the proposals and compares them using several simple criteria. The author further provides a few explanatory notes.

Probable Review Questions or Comments

Are these the most important evaluation criteria to consider or should we consider other points? Among these criteria, which is the most important? What is behind the "quality" ranking? Is it a subjective opinion or are there some sturdier evaluation criteria or analysis by an expert that supports this ranking? What results have been obtained by other companies using either the community college courses or the external resources? Who was involved in the consideration and assumption that internal resources could be diverted on short notice? What experience do they have with this sort of training in the past? What assumptions were made in assessing each alternative?

• Use internal resources to conduct a formal problem-solving program over the next several months.

Figure B.5

Suggestions to Consider

The author might consider adding additional criteria to the evaluation matrix or consider weighting the current criteria if one is significantly more important than the others. If any data exist to support the rankings, it might be provided in an additional attachment. Perhaps most importantly, the author will need to demonstrate that there is a good deal of consensus within the organization on the evaluation of alternatives and ultimate recommendation.

Recommendation

Strengths of the Section

This section (figure B.5) provides a simple statement recommending which of the alternatives the author would suggest in this instance. The statement is clear and easy for the audience to read.

Probable Review Questions or Comments

What is the main rationale for selecting this option? Why does the author reject the other options in favor of this one? What are the driving factors behind the recommendation? Were other departments or individuals involved in the selection and justification of this option? What is the time commitment and expertise required by an internal team, and who is best suited to undertake this sort of project? Has anyone been tentatively identified and approached about leading the course-development effort?

Suggestions to Consider

It is "best practice" in proposals to make it explicitly clear why a certain course of action is recommended. The author should consider ways to make the connection clearer between the alternatives and the recommendation. Proposal writing is not problem solving per se, and the link between cause and effect is usually demonstrated less in proposal writing because approval typically occurs before implementation actions are carried out. However, even proposals should strive to show clear linkages between any action items (or countermeasures) suggested and how they will affect the current condition.

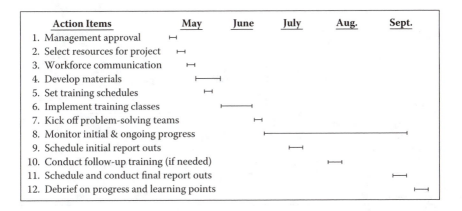

Figure B.6 Proposed timeline

Implementation Timeline

Strengths of the Section

The proposed timeline section (figure B.6) makes use of a timeline in conjunction with high-level implementation activities required to support the proposal. The chart outlines the general timing visually, and includes the Check and Act steps of the PDCA cycle.

Probable Review Questions or Comments

Which of the action items is likely to be the most difficult or most critical? What level of confidence lies behind these action items and the associated timelines? Who was involved in the generation of these items and the timing estimates? Is this timeline fast enough to launch pilots, learn from the review, and achieve the goals by the end of the year? On the other hand, are parts of it too aggressive (such as developing training materials and classes in just a few weeks)? How many resource hours in total will be required to support all this work, and are there any internal costs that are not being considered? Who is best suited to conduct this sort of work or has proper experience?

Suggestions to Consider

In proposals, the implementation plan is generally pretty high level. Before approval is granted, it is difficult to invest time in making plans that are very

Practical Problem Solving Training Proposal

Background

- Defects up 30+% over last 12 months in manufacturing
- Supervisor and lead person turnover in past 12 months is close to 50%
- Need to reduce defects to meet corporate goals set out for manufacturing operations in '07
- Opportunity to improve workforce skills and develop human resources in manufacturing

Current Condition

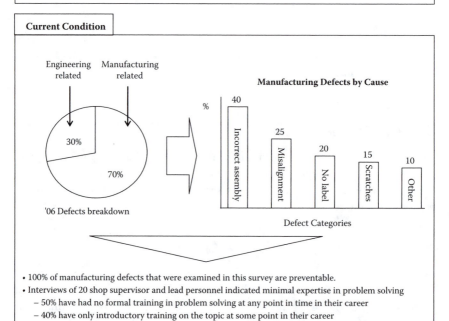

- 100% of manufacturing defects that were examined in this survey are preventable.
- Interviews of 20 shop supervisor and lead personnel indicated minimal expertise in problem solving
  - 50% have had no formal training in problem solving at any point in time in their career
  - 40% have only introductory training on the topic at some point in their career
  - 10% have had some more advanced training in their career and could provide examples

Proposal

- Implement a practical problem-solving training program over the next quarter in manufacturing
  - Reduce defects by over 50% by the end of the year in manufacturing
  - Improve the problem-solving capability of existing personnel

Figure B.7a   Practical Problem-Solving Training Proposal A3

From: Scott S.
To: Gary K.
Date: April 22, 2006

Evaluation of Alternatives

Alternatives	Criteria		
	Cost	*Quality*	*Timing*
A. Hire external resource for training and implementation	$40K	High	Mid-June
B. Utilize training at a local community college	$15K	Medium	June
C. Use internal resources and develop materials	N/A	Medium	May

Overall Comments:
- Target consultant group available and has proven experience with affiliate company in the area. However, they cannot support the training until mid-June due to resource constraints.
- Local community college course does not start until the June summer session begins and training would be off site. Follow-up support possible.
- Internal resources could be diverted on short notice. One person from training and development and one full-time resource from manufacturing would be required to support the training and roll-out.

Recommendation

- Use internal resources to conduct a formal problem solving program over the next several months.

Implementation Timeline

Action Items	May	June	July	Aug.	Sept.
1. Management approval	⊢				
2. Select resources for project	⊢				
3. Workforce communication	⊢				
4. Develop materials	⊢——⊣				
5. Set training schedules	⊢				
6. Implement training classes	⊢——⊣				
7. Kick off problem-solving teams		⊢			
8. Monitor initial & ongoing progress		⊢————————————⊣			
9. Schedule initial report outs			⊢		
10. Conduct follow-up training (if needed)				⊢	
11. Schedule and conduct final report outs				⊢	
12. Debrief on progress and learning points					⊢

Figure B.7b   Practical Problem-Solving Training Proposal A3

detailed. This timeline is probably a sufficient start for this purpose. It could be improved by identifying the responsible parties for each action item. This section could also add the estimated manpower hours or include a column that ranks the items by difficulty (such as easy, medium, hard).

Summary of A3 Report Review

The complete example proposal A3 is shown in figure B.7 for your reference and review. As in appendix A, we hope you get a sense of the importance of reviewing A3 reports. The act of writing in a structured manner causes authors to clarify their own thoughts for communication. In a similar fashion, reviewing A3s can lead to further insight, clarity of thought, and areas for improvement. Quite often, in the case of proposal writing, authors must refine their initial ideas as more data comes to light. This example could be a preliminary review, for example, that is either approved at this stage (depending upon the assumptions noted previously) or returned for more justification and revision. It depends on the circumstances—remember that we present this example only as a hypothetical case to think about for practice purposes.

The primary aim of this book is to provide an introduction to A3 report writing and the three basic types. The first step is to learn how to write the basic types and, of course, execute the work associated with them. In its simplest sense, this is nothing more than a tool to execute the PDCA cycle of management. The review process, whether during preliminary stages or at the latter report-out stages, is very important for the development of the individual as well as the organization.

As a final note, these appendix examples are just samples and not answers to which you want to cling. The secret within A3 reports is in the "thinking" part of equation and the continual ongoing development of personnel. We hope that you attempt to make use of this technique and further your own skills over time. Good luck!

Index

A

Act step, 4, 6, 19, 45, 60–61, 69–70, 88, 155
Action list, problem-solving A3 report, 42
Active voice, use of, *vs.* passive voice, 105–106
Advisor, discussion with, 80, 100–101
Aesthetics of report, 104
Alternative countermeasures in problem solving, 24
Amount of data, in graphics, 107
Approval, 121–123
   establishing convention for, 122–123
   levels of, 122
   need for, 122
   obtaining, 26
      proposal A3 report, 82–83
Articles published about Toyota, 1
Assumptions, confrontation of, 4
Audience, awareness of, problem-solving A3 report, 33–34

B

Background section, problem-solving A3 report, example, 34
Bar chart, 108
Bill drop time reduction sample problem-solving A3 report, 137–147
   background, 138–139
   cause analysis, 141–142
   check, 143–144
   countermeasures, 142–143
   current condition, 139–140
   follow-up, 144
   goal statement, 140–141
   summary, A3 report review, 145
Boldfacing, 106

Brainstorming changes to current system, 23–24
Brevity, to force synthesis of learning, 15–16, 104–105
Broad context, understanding situation in, 18
Bulleted lists, 105

C

Cafeteria food service recommendations example, proposal A3 report, 70–76
Caption, use in graphics, 107, 109
Cause, effect, discerning difference between, 12
Check step, 4–6, 19, 25, 59, 69
Clarification of problem, 21–22
Clarity of message in graphics, 107
Clutter, visual, in graphical materials, avoiding, 110–111
Coaching, for writing effective A3, 120–121
   comments by individuals, asking for, 120–121
   consultants, 121
   feedback, 120–121
   multiple source input, obtaining, 120–121
   problem-solvers in organization, counsel of, 121
Collaborative nature of A3 report system, 11–12
Comma usage in reports, 106
Communication efficacy, form, style, effect on, 103
Company goals, tying background to, problem-solving A3 report, 34
Computer-generated A3s, handwritten, compared, 117–120